Dear Olina
Wishing you a
lifetime of
peace!
Lots o

IT'S TOO HARD TO BE PERFECT

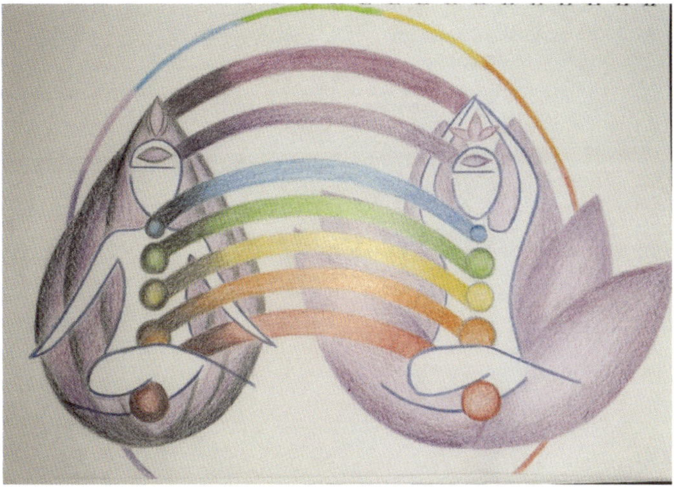

JANE SILVER

ISBN: 978-1-83556-002-0 PAPERBACK

ISBN: 978-1-83556-003-7 EBOOK

Book Design by HMDpublishing

About the Author

Jane started her working career at seventeen years old as a secretary in a Health Management Unit based at the University of Manchester. She spent 18 happy years working alongside the Human Resource Director, who saw something that made him send her back to University of Salford part-time, where she studied CIPD (Human Resource Management) and Psychology. After 17 years, she moved Departments where she worked with Medical students in the field of pastoral care and advice, gaining the trust of all whom she worked with on both personal and student matters.

It was whilst working there, that she discovered a real passion for helping to solve other people's dilemmas and problems and after seven years, took herself back to studying Counselling and therapeutic techniques, including Counselling and Hypnotherapy, Counselling and Psychotherapy, Neurolinguistic Programming, Psychometric

Testing and Analysis, Cognitive Behavioural Therapy, Emotional Freedom Technique, Mindfulness Based Inner Re-patterning, ACT Therapy, Yoga Therapy, Freeing adverse childhood experience, Somatic Therapy, Time Line and Gestalt Therapy. This culminated in her completing ILM Level 7 (Masters Level Equivalent) in Life and Business Coaching, Leadership, Management, Mentoring, Mindfulness and Mediation.

It's an unusual combination incorporating, Human Resources, Business Management, Psychotherapy, Counselling and Energy Psychology but in doing so, Jane is now one of only a handful of coaches that can assist anybody, whatever their situation across the whole coaching continuum.

In 2009 she opened the doors to a private integrated psychodynamic counselling practice which continues to go from strength to strength with clients coming from all over the world. She has in the past volunteered her time to Childline School Service and to the Bury District Citizens Advice Bureau. More recently, she volunteers her time to the Heads Up Charity (Looking at creating the 4th emergency service in psychological trauma care!) following the Manchester Evening News Arena attack, Grenfell Tower and London Bridge attacks.

Forward

This book is written with the help and inspiration of many special people who weren't afraid to show their vulnerability and ask for help and assistance.They have taught me as much as I have taught them and for that I am truly grateful.

Naturally, all their identities remain anonymous but they know who they are and I'm proud of every single of one of them for making their journey :). and agreeing to be part of this book.

The inspiration for "It's Too Hard To Be Perfect" came from them.This book aims to share stories and impart some of the tools and coping techniques that were used to help them.

It is written precisely for them and for others who seek answers to questions, that they can't get their heads around.

Each chapter aims to impart a small snapshot that shows that perfectionism is subjective and even though we may strive for flawlessness, our critical selves are full of multiple layers and dimensions. Connecting the dots to find our true happiness is unique to each individual, but we need to be looking internally not externally for the answers. Our behaviour is influenced by our own thoughts, urges and memory in three aspects of our psyche, the ID, Ego and Superego and these are driven by pleasure, morals, instincts, judgement and are repulsed by pain. Our brains operate in different formats or operating systems, known as representational systems and we programme them according to our beliefs and values. Understanding basic psychology helps with stress management, decision making and in seeing all aspects of human behaviour opening the mind to different perspectives and possibility. Colour has the capacity to heal emotional upheaval, health conditions and mental stress. We only have to see a rainbow in the dark sky after its been raining and it helps us to lighten up and feel brighter. Life is one big drama! What do people think of me? Who am I? Why am I so pre-occupied with issues of identity or comparison.

Young people and teenagers today are dealing with many complex issues and often struggle to find any answers. Hopefully, "It's too Hard To be Perfect" will go along way to explaining some of them. My advice would always be to seek the support of an adult whom you trust, get professional support if you need to (no stigma attached to it these days!) and definitely get everyone you know (including parents and teachers to read it too!)

If you are feeling worried or scared, frightened or anxious, angry or sad. You are not sleeping, not eating, struggling at School/College/University or even work. Or are being bullied, experiencing grief or have an addiction or phobia please help yourself to this book. It is full of coping strategies to help deal with many everyday problems. As parents we are not given a manual to deal with our children's difficulties. I wish we were!

Each chapter is clearly marked, has a real life case study and beautiful illustrations, cleverly designed to bring this book and my words to life!

All the exercises can all be used separately or in conjunction with one another and have all been tried and tested by the story tellers themselves and many more of my clients.

The strategies can be used throughout life into adulthood. When the tough gets going and at some point it will, please remember it's "Too Hard To be Perfect".

Enjoy!

Contents

CHAPTER 1
What is perfect? Does it exist? **10**

CHAPTER 2
Connecting the dots of your unique canvas of life. **18**

CHAPTER 3
The Brain and how it functions - basic neuropsychological education **23**

CHAPTER 4
The ID, The Ego and the Superego - what is this all about. **32**

CHAPTER 5
Neuro-linguistic Representational Systems - What are they and Why are they so Important. **36**

CHAPTER 6
Are We Programming our Computers with Negative Language with the help of those that we trust implicitly. Teachers beware!! Can we change the programme like we change the TV Channels? **41**

CHAPTER 7
A Little Bit of Basic Psychology - Our Personal Iceberg and our Basic Needs explained **44**

CHAPTER 8
Food and its Challenges **49**

CHAPTER 9
Emoticons and our Emotions **53**

CHAPTER 10
Who or What is Perfect? - Body Image, Self Esteem and Building Confidence **59**

CHAPTER 11
Grief and Trauma **64**

CHAPTER 12
Addictions and Phobia's **76**

CHAPTER 13
A little bit about colour **87**

CHAPTER 14
Life and it's drama **90**

CHAPTER 15
A brief understanding of some of the different therapeutic techniques and how they are used to help. **94**

CHAPTER 16
Concluding thoughts. **108**

Chapter 1

What is perfect? Does it exist?

Perfect is just a perception of how we think we ought to be and what is perfect for someone, is certainly not perfect for someone else. Perfectionism is about believing that self-worth is based on achievement and often stems from high, rigid, critical or shaming parental or teacher expectation.

Imperfect however is the same as I'm perfect. Interestingly, the only thing that separates them is a hard working little apostrophe mark! Apostrophe marks symbolise possession which can hold an emotional connection to who we are and what we value. They also show clarity which as a self concept can refer to our identity, our qualities and how consistent and confident we are with them. The apostrophe also replaces a missing letter but if we're missing a piece then we need to find it. How can we find perfectionism if it's subjective?

My understanding or perception of reaching anywhere near perfect is an impossible never ending task. Leaving ego's aside (see Chapter 4 The ID, The Ego and the Superego!). When we think we've accomplished something and feel proud, something just around the corner can come along and take that away.

We travel along different paths, seeking our idea of perfection, but inevitably at some point we'll get stuck, feel lost or alone on our journey. We can feel angry to protect ourselves from the sadness we're feeling, or anxious that things are not going how we expect.

Each and everyone of us is different though and in order to find our own unique human journey, we must find acceptance.

Think of the inside of your whole body like a maze, with many different, tunnels, connections, fascia, chemical reactions and cells. To make individuals whole (to be the best version of themselves they can be), they need to connect each section like an extremely complex dot to dot. If one piece of the puzzle isn't joined or a bit is missing, we cannot be whole.

We need to make sure we feel physically well. To do that we need to have strong immunity, we need to move, we need to sleep well and eat a balanced diet including many vitamins and phytonutrients so we can be strong and grow (not just physically, but mentally too!). We need to have all of our basic human needs met, including food, water, shelter and breath, we need to feel safe and secure but if we feel insecure our subconscious being doesn't feel safe. We need to find our tribe, whether that is in a community, a family unit, at a club or a gym or in a friendship circle, we need to feel like we belong. Once all the above are being met, we can build our self worth and confidence and finally reach the goal of being the best version of ourselves that we can be, but that doesn't necessarily mean perfect. (Maslow hierarchy of needs).

We need to make sure we are resilient to the ups and downs of life. We must feel safe and secure and like we belong in order to have that resilience. Unfortunately, though life is full of complexities, grief, loss, trauma, change, expectation, belief (some of which doesn't even belong to us), and actually, just learnt from peers, friends and family members.

We need to feel connected to the whole picture. We have to learn how our mind, body and soul are an important part of the bigger picture and then we may just find what is just perfect for us. Please remember though that what is perfect for us as an individual won't work for someone else. We need to take into account our life values and beliefs, our perspective of what we want to achieve, what ultimately makes us feel safe and feel inner peace and what gives us the strength and resilience to ride life's waves. It wouldn't do for us all to be like each other and want the same things out of life. It's the canvas of people and their little imperfections that make the world work as it does. Remember not all stories end with a happy ever after, I wish they did but think of life's journey as different chapters of your own book that you can change and alter accordingly. Remember we can't change the past and we can't write the future otherwise we'd all be very rich!!

What have I learnt along my journey?

As a therapist with extensive experience, I have learnt many things some of which have truly blown my mind. Ultimately, I never imagined in my wildest dreams that if emotional blockages are cleared often so is the physical ailment or disease that binds them. The mind is truly the most powerful computer in the world and working within it, is both fascinating and daunting all at once. Each and every mind is perfect and just the way its meant to be.

On many occasions during therapy I've had the privilege to listen to many emotional stories and the journeys that individuals have taken. Spinning the perspective and helping clients to look inwards instead of outwards for help has made the hugest difference to them. I have witnessed with my own eyes pain disappearing, fibromyalgia melting away week by week, tingling sensations of energy actually moving instead of staying stuck, breath deepening enabling lungs to do a better job and on one such occasion a tumour shrank - later confirmed by an MRI scan and disbelief from the consultant declaring it a miracle case. The very root of the trauma released hence the mass collapsing. My belief is that miracles do happen with a little help and assistance but most of all with hope and mindset. If we take away hope from anybody or anything the journey to recovery becomes much more complicated. Never lose hope and never let anyone else take hope away from you.

I want to share here what I have learnt about striving for perfection as I look at everything from a wide angled lens, rather than from a narrow view finder and definitely from the inside out and not the outside in.

1. Underlying every difficulty there is an emotion that's stuck in the system. It's stuck in the very heart of who we are and what we stand for. A stuck emotion grows and often causes physical symptoms. E-Motion is energy in motion.
2. There is a solution to every challenge despite the most rigid of belief systems if we look in the right place and change the belief or the mindset.
3. Looking from the inside out, rather than the outside in, is the biggest lesson I can pass on. We are taught to look for external validation everywhere, but if the inside is not happy, no mask will help, however hard we try. The media in general, Instagram, TikTok, fashion magazines, the culture of externalising beauty doesn't help us to feel worthy, if anything it sensationalises and accentuates what we don't have rather than what we do.
4. Colour in all its forms, is truly healing. Fashion make-up, food, nature, flowers. If we eat bland processed food, we

feel bland, if we stay inside, we feel trapped inside literally, if we wear all black, we feel the darkness. Conversely if we wear colour we feel colourful, if we eat fruit and vegetables, we feel bright, if we walk in nature looking at the beauty of life we feel grateful. What I never realised is that integrating all this information truly makes a difference to our mental and physical health.

5. Energy is fundamentally the missing part of the jigsaw puzzle of human life and our very being. If we have no energy caused by an overwhelming blocked emotional overload or it's stagnant, then life is a struggle in every aspect. Energy blocks up in the Chakras. (Energetic pools/wheels/cogs). We have a pool in our throat that if blocked can stop us expressing ourselves either to others or inwardly to our very soul. The next pool is in our heart. If blocked this can cause heartache, panic, sadness and loss. This can ultimately affect relationships with both self and others. The next pool sits in our gut. (Gut reaction, gut feeling etc). If it's blocked here, we struggle with digestive issues, can feel bloated or like we've been punched in the stomach. Our pelvic region, responsible for our metabolism and sexual function also holds a pool and this is where our fear centre also sits. If it's blocked it can stop us from moving forwards, from reproducing and it affects our metabolic rate. A pool and blockage in the feet stops us from being grounded, destabilises us and stops us from moving forwards on the journey of life. The puzzle gets distorted and our perception to everything narrows.

6. If we have learnt behaviour and it doesn't represent who we are in line with our values then we can unlearn it. We don't need or nor should we follow someone else's path.

7. Labels of any description don't define who we are but we will look to seek out evidence to make us believe

that, that label is helping us in some way even if that belief doesn't make any sense.

8. Medication can in many ways help but sometimes it hinders our progress, to heal and isn't always the right answer. As an example, many of my clients take antidepressant medication but often they comment that "they're not really helping me"! Meanwhile, there is a part of them that still feels low that they can't shake away- which is the evidence that the subconscious needs to prove that they are in fact depressed and that feeling remains stuck in the hope that something will change. Unless we look at the root of where that issue first began and why the viscous cycle remains in the cogs of their very own downfall, the subconscious will do its best to protect us and often succeeds when the programme that it's written is stuck in its very own loop.

9. If we always repeat what we've always done then the answer will never change.

10. It's amazing how literal are bodies are. If we lose our sight for example we need to look at what we don't want to see in our life. If our hearing goes it may be wise to begin by listening to what we don't want to hear. A client of mine was suffering terribly with on-going migraine headaches. She'd visited every doctor and specialist and no-one really understood what was wrong as all the medical tests proved clear. I asked her who or what was causing her head to ache? As I asked her that question you could see physically that she was already more relaxed, the penny had dropped and she wanted to know and understand more. She had a lot going on, both at University and in her personal life and as a result, was extremely stressed.

    I taught her basic breathing techniques, how to do emotional freedom technique, (a percussive tapping technique on the acupressure points to release emotional overload), how to ground herself and to look within her own body for the answers she desperately wanted to find. Her body was definitely keeping the score with its own unique language and once it was de-coded and she had a better understanding of herself - in other words, how to read it, her migraines disappeared. She was convinced she had some terrible disease and yes she did have dis-ease in the head but the migraines were just a way for her body to let her know that someone or something was causing her head to ache!! Literally.

11. No amount of talking about feelings can release them, if they are stuck behind the cogs. Integrating somatic therapy, energy therapy with psychology, emotional freedom technique, inner-re-patterning and the emotion code will all help to do that.
12. We have a choice how to react and respond despite sometimes not feeling like we do.
13. Flexibility is key for both our minds and our bodies. It helps with resilience, change and growth.
14. Artificial intelligence is here and happening but no robot can substitute human behaviour and empathy.
15. We can't solve any issue looking in the wrong place. If our subconscious is holding onto a stuck belief or story and we try to solve it consciously, we will ultimately fail. This is because the two parts of the brain are working off completely different operating systems.
16. Those that matter really don't mind and those that mind really don't matter!

17. To achieve success follow the anagram below.

    S - Sense of Direction

    U - Understanding

    C - Courage

    C - Care

    E - Esteem

    S - Self Confidence

    S - Self Acceptance

Chapter 2

Connecting the dots of your unique canvas of life.

The mind, body and soul are not separate entities of our being. They are very much intertwined as one. They work hand in hand moving together like cogs of a giant game of downfall.

Downfall is an interesting connection because it is the very fact that we separate our mind, body and spirit that in the end becomes our very own downfall.

Unfortunately, we believe them to be separate as all evidence in the world, as we see it now (our reality) is pointing in that direction.

You go to a doctor's surgery with a bad stomach for example and leave with medication to help relieve the symptoms of that pain and trust that information to be fact. What if though that fact is taken from a small perspective or looked at through a small lens.

If that stomach pain is connected to a deep seated emotion that's stuck within the walls of our energetic system, then we need to root out what's stuck. Medication will mask the pain (perhaps temporarily) but the root is still very much there, building in the underground system of our being.

You read a newspaper article and take what we read as absolute fact but whose viewfinder is that article written?

You go to school and learn a syllabus that has been created in order for us to move through the journey of life but that syllabus doesn't suit every lens. We are full of complexities and sometimes no matter how hard we try, we can't put a square peg into a round hole or vice versa. It sometimes becomes an impossible task and drains our energetic function to even try to "fit in" in what is perceived to be the canvas that is for everyone - but sometimes we need to view it from a different lens, a completely different perspective. It becomes too hard to be perfect in a lens that doesn't suit our being, our beliefs or our values.

As humanity has developed and demands increase, we compromise our basic human needs which help our internal systems to thrive. Disturbed sleep affects our circadian rhythms, lack of nutrition affects our energy and resistance to illness. Eating the wrong foods at the wrong time impacts our glucose levels, moods and hormones. If we pay closer attention to our basic needs when analysing perceived problems, we can get to the root cause and choose the best way to move forward in a healthy way to flourish and not just exist. The brain constantly rewires itself to suit the information we feed it so if we constantly complain or find excuses it will find the evidence it needs to make that the reality.

The root of anything is where you need to be looking in order to become the best version of yourself. The house in which you reside (your body) can if you listen to it, provide you with everything you need to feel confident, self assured and empowered. To feel and be loved and to forgive and be compassionate. If you don't listen to its whispers, you may very well hear it scream! The more you are comfortable and connected to your house, a vessel in which you live and looking at it from an internal perspective, the more you begin to understand that aesthetics are only on the surface.

Later in the book, I bring your attention to "The Personal Iceberg" where, the surface is what the human eye sees but no-one is looking underneath in the underground.

Have we been taught to look in the wrong place? Are we using incorrect evidence? We always look for evidence to prove to ourselves that we are right, but we will always be drawn to a "self fulfilling prophecy" so if we believe something to be true, rightly or wrongly that's where the evidence will draw us. Round in a vicious circle.

All the systems of the body as I've mentioned before are hugely interlinked and work like cogs of a huge machine, to carry nutrition and oxygen, to break our food down absorbing what is necessary to help the body to work optimally, but if we struggle to break down the particles perhaps due to indigestible emotional overload then our health can be adversely affected.

Hormones are like little messengers that help with our metabolism, emotional regulation, promoting growth and keeping our temperature in check. Hormonal imbalances are common but if the endocrine system gets stuck we can feel stressed, frustrated and confused and often out of balance.

Our immune system helps to keep us free from bacteria and viruses and any other foreign aid that our body believes is unsafe. It will not function to its optimum if we feel inner conflict or are generally insecure.

Our lymphatic drainage system, does exactly that, it removes excess fluid from our tissues and helps our antibodies to do their job.When we are unable to drain the excess fluids because of strong feelings of fear, vulnerability, rejection and not feeling loved, our thymus, lymph glands and spleen can be adversely affected.

Our muscles help our bodies to move, supporting us through movement, strength and flexibility but when we carry extra tension and stress, burdens of responsibility, fear and weaknesses then muscles cannot work to their optimum.

I'm sure you can see now that we are connected but it is the nervous system, that is the internal link (through the vagus nerve) that connects and brings together our internal and external worlds transmitting information. If the vagus nerve isn't stable it will run between fight, flight and freeze, believing or perceiving it to be protecting us, but ultimately it will break down because of stress, negative thoughts and internal conflict.

The respiratory system helps to eliminate waste and helps us to breathe. If we struggle to breathe because of a blocked emotion of hatred, grief or anger or not feeling worthy or being unable to communicate what we truly feel, we gasp for air literally.

All our bodily systems connect emotion, to feelings, to sensations through to our central nervous system, which ultimately sends a signal to the brain to say we're not safe. Protect us. It's never meant to cause harm and its ultimate aim is survival which is a primary human function. Survival however, is not a quality existence. It's much more beneficial for us to thrive.

Connecting the dots will always be impossible if you are looking in the wrong direction. The dots are always internal as the next story brings to our attention.

A beautiful young woman, was lost and confused, she was indeed looking in the wrong place to connect her dots. She wasn't listening to her own self and was negatively impacted by hiding herself behind what she believed or perceived everyone else thought of her. She was using self sabotage as a coping technique. Anytime anyone said anything nice, she rejected it, she never could ask for help despite sometimes needing it, pushing away anyone that tried to get close and refusing to try something unless she could do it perfectly, constantly criticising and isolating herself which hurt her more. She was emotionally overwhelmed, with blockages in insecurity, fear, and loss. Feeling this, she moved so far away from her beliefs and values that creating a new persona to protect herself, seemed subconsciously like her only option, which then took her off piste. Once she connected her dots, she felt hope for her future and excitement for the next part of her journey. She now has a different understanding and a new canvas - a different lens or view finder. The generation that follows her will now not need to hold onto the anxiety and depression she's felt that was stuck in her pathway, stopping her from moving forwards.

Chapter 3

The Brain and how it functions - basic neuropsychological education

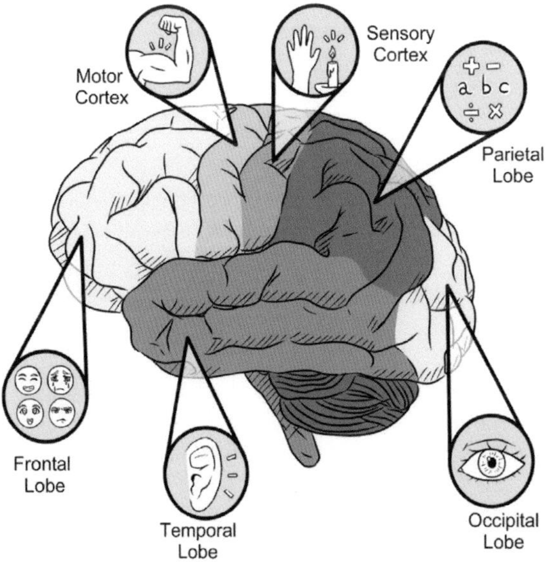

Our Brains are very complex and even Neuroscientists don't know everything about how they function 100% of the time. It is very important though, from a basic perspective that we understand how it functions.

Our brain is the main organ or muscle in our Central Nervous System and is situated in our skull. It also covers certain bones in our face and three small bones within our ears. The brain stem actually comes from behind the ear and not from the base of the neck like we would imagine. Scientists know that the right side of the brain controls the left side of the body and the left side of the brain controls the right side of the body so its a bit back to front or a mirror image.

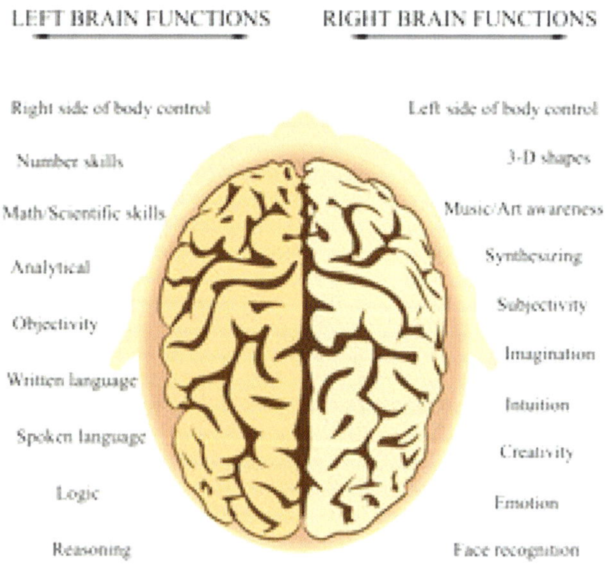

All parts of our Central Nervous System including our brain are connected by nerves, wires or neurones that lead via the spinal cord which runs down our backs and is protected by the vertebrae. The wires connect together to create signals, chemicals, hormones and impulses. There are twelve cranial nerves in total each doing the relevant job to send messages to keep us moving, safe and alive.

If we were to split each section of our brains up into different compartments or jigsaw pieces then we can see clearly how it all works together. See diagram above

Our **Frontal Lobe** is responsible for our thinking and planning functions, how we organise and problem solve, how we control our emotions, personality and our behaviour. Our **Motor Cortex** is responsible for how we move, our **Sensory Cortex** responsible for our sensations. We have a lobe called **Parietal Lobe** which is responsible for how we make sense of everything, how we perceive things to be and how students learn how to spell and how to do maths. Our **Occipital Lobe** is responsible for our sight and our **Temporal Lobe** how we understand, use language and also responsible for our memory.

At the entrance to our Frontal Lobe buried between that and the Temporal lobe, we have something called the **Amygdala.** It's almond in shape and I always like to explain to my clients young and old, that if we were to put flappy ears and a face onto the almond shaped Amygdala then we have something that resembles a "guard dog". Our dog is primarily there to protect us from danger or harm and to look after us but what would happen if the dog was frightened or worried, anxious or scared about something?

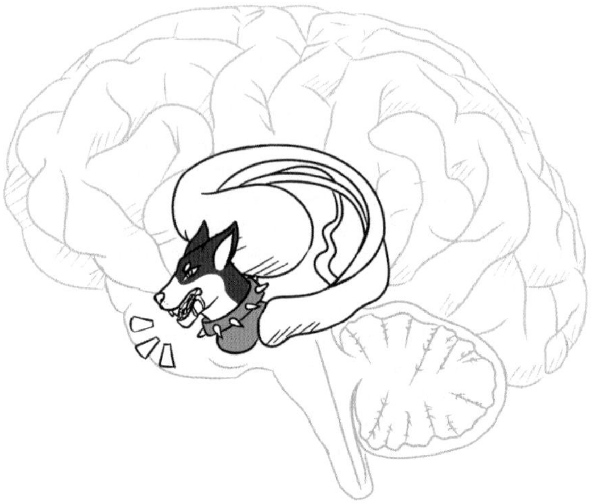

The dog would bark permanently until it wasn't scared or frightened any longer.

This is how the human fight or flight response works. If we are permanently frightened, worried or scared our guard dog springs into action and barks incessantly. It kicks over our frontal lobe responsible for how we think, plan and organise. It destabilises us.

The Amygdala (fight, flight, freeze response) is connected to the poly vagal system, which is part of the autonomic nervous system that helps to regulate all of our basic bodily functions. This system has three of the twelve cranial nerves attached to it. The ventral nerve, running down the front and into the Central Nervous System. This is responsible for how we know how to run away or fight, if we find ourselves in a dangerous situation. The Dorsal nerve, running down the back and connected to our older amphibian brain. This is responsible for how we freeze (play dead) like the amphibians in the wild when in danger. The vagus nerve wanders in the centre, connecting how we think and feel. If the vagus nerve is at all destabilised then our bodies will automatically go into fight, flight and freeze. The good news is that the vagus nerve is a muscle like every other muscle in our body and can be exercised to re-stabilise itself. Tasks throughout this book, are primarily there for vagal toning and exercise so we can feel much more balanced, less stressed and calm.

Our fight, flight, freeze system has many physical reactions. Excess adrenaline is secreted into our bodies, to help us to prepare to run away. This is closely followed, by the stress hormone cortisol. Imagine this hormone is like sticky, thick black treacle toffee. Once this is in our system, our respiration rates need to increase, along with our heart rate, blood pressure and sugar levels. Our muscles tense up, our digestion gets inhibited, our blood thickens and hearing can even become sensitised. It also has an emotional connection. Our perspective narrows and we tend to live in the future or in the past. We can take risk and isolate ourselves. Our internal dialogue becomes should I have done this, or if only I would have done that and then our reactions and responses become exaggerated.

If we yo-yo between living in fight and flight or fight, flight and freeze or if we get stuck, then we end up activating the permanent fight, flight, freeze response which can be like setting off a false alarm. What if I told you though, that you can switch that false alarm off manually, by sending a morse code message to that part of the brain using your breath? Amazing news - right?? Start by breathing into your belly for three counts, hold at the top for four counts as if you're holding your breath and then exhale for five as if breathing out a big sigh of relief. Repeat three times. This ultimately sends a message to the Amygdala that we are safe and not in any danger, hence no need for a false ringing alarm. Our brains are smart, but they have a flaw - they cannot tell the difference between what is real, perceived or what is imagined.

Yo-yoing can cause many health issues that range from headaches, loss of sleep, panic attacks and a whole host of other feelings, sensations and behaviours that we don't know, understand or are taught how to manage. This leaves our Frontal lobe and all its functions in a state of confusion, unable to think properly, to organise or manage, which then in turn affects our ability to control our emotions, personality and our behaviour.

It's a bit like a filing cabinet that at the beginning is in perfect order, neat and concise. Then somebody comes and flips the filing cabinet over, leaving all the files inside in a mess, in no order and where it becomes difficult to find anything. Our brains react in a similar way, leaving us with essentially a gap or empty space where nothing is rational, we can't think straight and we do things that are out of character.

Anxiety is a growing problem and it is important that we teach everyone how to manage their problems and not avoid them. Avoidance often makes things worse.

TASK:-

FEEL is a great anagram that helps us to remember what to do when we or someone close to us is feeling anxious.

F = FREEZE. STOP AND BREATHE DEEPLY RIGHT DOWN TO THE BELLY. THROUGH THE NOSE AND OUT THROUGH THE MOUTH.

WHY DO WE NEED TO STOP AND BREATHE.

A word about breathing!!

To breathe is an automatic and also an autonomous function that we can control. When we worry, we're frightened or scared, we breathe from the top of our chests and usually shallowly. When we deepen it and control it we feel calmer. It's the perfect way to exercise the vagus nerve to manually take us out of that fight, flight freeze response.

It helps to alter both our mental and physical states working through the nervous system to help it feel calm enabling it to relax.

If we are taught to mindfully breathe, it reduces stress and anxiety, alters the amount of oxygen helping our internal organs and can even lower our blood pressure helping the heart.

Mindful breathing techniques can be used anywhere. An Interesting fact regarding anyone vaping or smoking. Think of the sheer action of taking an inhale of a vape or cigarette. Inhaling a deep breath in, holding it before exhaling out. It's the very act of breathing that helps them to relax - not the vape or cigarette!! Those that practice mindfully breathing, those that meditate or those that do yoga are generally much less stressed.

E = EMPATHISE. ENSURING THAT EVERYONE KNOWS HOW YOU FEEL

Empathy goes a long way. Try to understand that each and every person has a point of view and if you can understand that point of view from their perspective rather than your own, that can hugely help. You may even be able to sense or physically feel another persons feelings.

E = EVALUATE THE SITUATION AND THEN TRY AND FIGURE OUT THE BEST SOLUTION OR DIFFERENT OPTIONS.

If someone near to you is struggling with anxiety or panic tell them to breathe deeply into the pit of the stomach, hold it and then release it as if they are blowing out a big purposeful sigh of relief.

L = LET GO

Please remember that worrying is a natural gift that has a purpose. It is a protection mechanism but sometimes it can set off just like a false alarm. It's the false alarm that causes unnecessary anxiety.

Please don't ignore the feeling of anxiety. Try bringing it to life as a character. This helps our brains response by putting the logical brain back in order.

Feelings are like clouds. If we were to jump up and touch a cloud it would disappear into vapour. Please remember that feelings come and go just like the clouds. They are not permanent.

Try imagining that thoughts are like bubbles. Reach out and catch one of them. Does it change as you think about it.

Anxious people tend to think in the future but our brains are great at travelling through time. Instead of asking what if, try living in the present and ask what is.

Please don't use the avoidance technique. I won't do this because it makes me anxious, unfortunately, this just makes the anxiety worse. Anxiety always seeks evidence and if you give it the evidence it needs it will feed off it. Instead try chunking (breaking goals down into manageable chunks) with the aim of reaching your goal. Think of it as climbing a ladder one step at a time until you get to the top.

Chapter 4

The ID, The Ego and the Superego - what is this all about.

Understanding the ID, EGO and Super Ego. Sigmund Freud's understanding of human personality which in turn affects complex human behaviour.

Freuds structural model of human personality is split into three.

ID - Child

Ego - Parent

Superego - Grandparent.

The ID

This part of the brain helps us to drive our behaviour. However, it is primitive, and illogical, and incorporates irrational, impulsive, and instinctive thinking processes which can be child like. The ID is extremely head strong and often stubborn. Think of a small child that demands an ice cream, before they've eaten their tea. They can scream and shout and perform until that demand is met. If that demand is met immediately then the Ego doesn't understand how to balance its responsibility.

The Ego

The Ego's responsibility is to balance out the needs of the Child and the demands of reality. The Ego is part of the ID but has been influenced from the external world and therefore it's been modified. This part of the brain can mediate between the unrealistic child (ID) and the real world basing its decision making on our personalities and reasoning. Unlike its counterpart the ID, that is both unreasonable and chaotic.

The Ego is able to operate within principles working out realistic and satisfying demands but avoiding negative consequences. It seeks pleasure like the ID to reduce any pain or tension but does so using more realistic strategies, despite the fact that it doesn't know the difference between right or wrong. Something is good if it achieves what it requires without causing any harm to itself or the ID.

Freud made the analogy that the Ego is like a man on horseback who has to hold onto the superior strength of the (ID) horse.

If the Ego fails in its attempt to use the reality principle then unconscious defence or coping mechanisms are employed to help ward off any unpleasant feelings. (Anxiety)

The Ego then has to engage in secondary process thinking to help problem solve.

The Super Ego

This part of the brain is looking for moral perfection. It incorporates the values and morals (learned behaviour) of our parents, peers, friends and develops between the ages of 3 - 5.

It's function is to control the IDs child like impulses, especially those that society forbids and it's function is to persuade the Ego to turn to more moralistic goals.

It has two systems. The conscience and the Ideal self.

The conscience can punish the Ego through causing feelings of guilt.

For example. If the Ego gives into the IDs demands the superego may make the person feel bad through guilt

The Ego- ideal or ideal self is an imaginary picture of how you think you ought to be.

Behaviour which we believe falls short of the ideal self may be punished by the superego through guilt. The superego can also reward us through the ideal self when we behave 'properly' by making us feel proud.

What happens though if our ideal self is too high of a standard - then whatever a person does will represent failure.

The ideal self and conscience are largely determined in childhood from parental values and how we are brought up.

It is the idealistic super-ego present in the conscious brain, the pre conscious and the unconscious that drives the ego's demands for greater perfection. It is the very conflicts and interactions between these three components that create our personalities. Ultimately it is the internal conflict, internal pressure and overwhelm and the desire to avoid failure (even though failure doesn't exist - its just lessons learnt!) or to be judged that drives the psychoanalytical theory of "perfectionism".

Perfectionism alone is neutral but when a belief or mindset becomes so rigid and seeks unrealistic goals and standards that are impossible to achieve it becomes toxic to the mind, body and soul, resulting in burnout and failed relationships.

Chapter 5

Neuro-linguistic Representational Systems - What are they and Why are they so Important.

What are our Representational Systems? Everyone has a different representational system and because of this everyone's representation of perfect is different.

How we understand the world is based solely on what we sense, what we see, hear, and feel, smell and taste. That's usually the only bit of information that we can get hold of because humans can only pay conscious attention to between 5 and 9 bits of the 11 million bits of sensory information that we receive every minute. That's a lot of information!! Our unconscious mind therefore has to process, ignore, generalise and then delete information before we really even know about it, when it reaches our conscious mind.

Our main unconscious filters include:

Visual - How we See - 40% of the population -

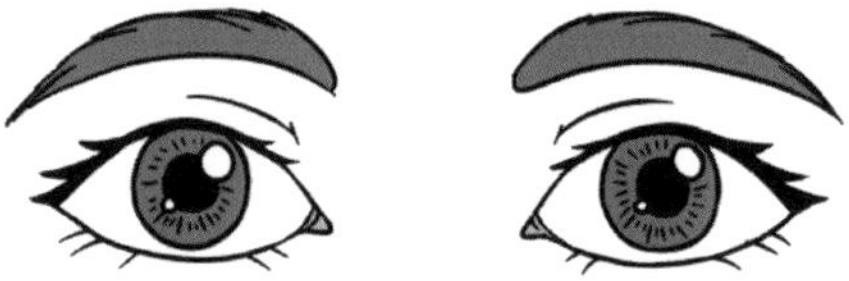

Auditory Tonal- How we Hear - 10% of the population-

Kinaesthetic - How we Feel - our Emotions, 40% of the population-

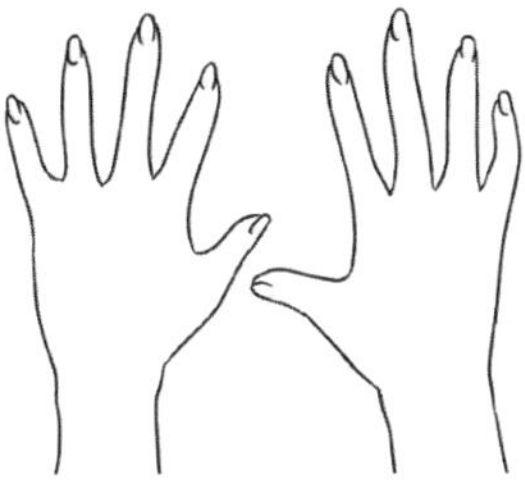

AD - Auditory Digitals - 10% of the population. Computer Brains-

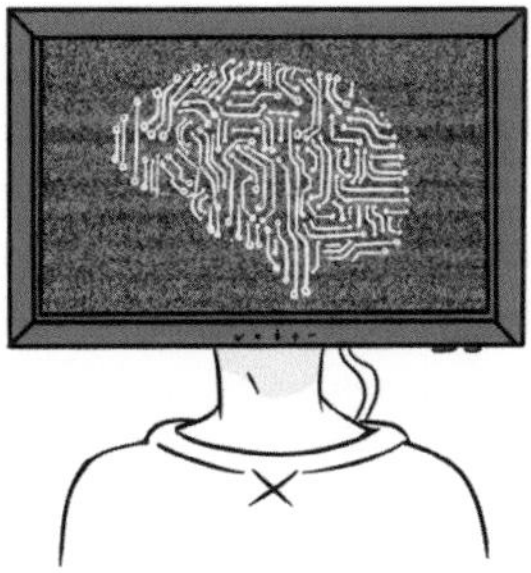

Olfactory - Our sense of Smell –

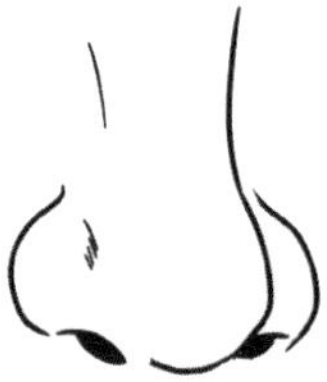

Gustatory - Our Tastes-

This is the language we use each and everyday.

Meta Programming to include the type of personalities we have and the way in which we choose to programme our information.

Our Memory Archive is important to what we have experienced in the past and our belief systems and values show us what we believe to be true and important. This is usually learned from our Trusted Adults, Peers, Teachers and Parents, Carers or Guardians.

Each and everyone of us uses our five senses on a moment to moment basis but the level of importance based on the information that we receive varies widely between person to person. So for example, someone may have a preferred Kinaesthetic representational system over someone who has a preferred visual one. This makes each individual see things from a different view point or mind set.

Why are they so Important?

If we are spoken to by peers, parents, teachers etc in a representational system that doesn't match our own, then we may as well be conversing in a different language. Take someone who is highly auditory digital. Think in terms of a computer programme - everything is black and white and organised with little or no emotion attached to the task in hand. Instruction manuals are read precisely and taken literally. For people who are visual and kinaesthetic on the other hand, they don't necessarily see in black and white. Everything is much more coloured. They prefer to see and feel their way around a problem or task and follow diagrams as opposed to written instruction. They are much more emotional and can burst into tears easily and sometimes for no apparent reason. Take a look around at some of your friends, peers, teachers etc. Try to guess their representational system and chances are you will get along much more easily with those that have the same system as you. Teachers included!! The reason that this happens is because for those that have different systems, they are having to work twice as hard to get themselves understood because they are effectively speaking in foreign languages to each other. Think of it as a radio frequency. We've set the programme to a particular station but we go out of the area. What happens next is we end up with a frequency that's not clear or a bit muffled. Meta programming works in a similar way so for example, if a kinaesthetic person and an auditory digital person are working together, it can become difficult to manage due to the poor frequency.

If our knowledge and understanding of these systems were understood more widely then communication between different people becomes more expandable (helping us to look from a different view point!) and enabling us to pick up on the missing links blurred by the distorted frequency!

Take the questionnaire in the NLP section of this book to establish which representational system you are and then give it to your friends and family. It may just help with communication.

Chapter 6

Are We Programming our Computers with Negative Language with the help of those that we trust implicitly. Teachers beware!! Can we change the programme like we change the TV Channels?

The human brain is the most powerful computer in the world but most humans use just 10% of its capacity and many don't use it to its best advantage. Most of our behaviour works on auto pilot and because of this our brains are very much taken for granted. Perhaps our personal deep seated thoughts, interpretation of those thoughts and assumption helps us to judge and make decisions contributing to that behaviour, but what if they are subconscious and therefore unconditionally bias? We don't really understand how much information we absorb on a day to day basis but we filter it according to our own canvas.

If we programme our computer brain with negative information, then we are obviously going to get a negative response. How many of you tell yourselves on a regular basis that you are 'not good enough, you're too fat, you don't like this or that about yourselves, you're going to fail! etc. You wouldn't dream about telling your best mate that they're not good enough, so why tell yourself. It's effectively bullying your very own soul.

How many of you can hear that voice that is pulling you apart with negative speak, making your glass definitely half empty as opposed to half full? If this sounds familiar, then your computer programme needs wiping clean to reverse the negative patterns. What if someone inadvertently tells you, you're not good enough? Or that you're a bit overweight etc. We may believe that to be true and then our brain looks for the evidence to match that.

Our life experiences, beliefs and values create our thought patterns. Our thought patterns create our emotions, our emotions create physical symptoms, (headaches, nausea, stomach problems, blood pressure, panic attacks to name a few), which then leads us to use avoidance strategies. (If we feel nausea, we don't eat, we then create body confidence issues etc… is just one example).

What if….. we could change our negative thought pattern to a positive one?

Unbelievably, our brains are so clever that it is possible to change the pattern just like switching sides on a TV channel.

TASK

Imagine that you are putting your whole life story on a big TV or computer screen. Imagine that you have an imaginary remote control in your hand.

Watch your life story unfold from as far back as you can remember to present day. If it gets difficult you can pause the video with the imaginary remote control or even switch it off. If you do need to pause it or switch it off, try and understand what feeling or sensation was making it uncomfortable for you. Watch until the end if you can and then rewind it back to the beginning and watch for a second time. Your brain is aware of what you are attempting to do now, so the second time, the stories of your life may appear more vivid, or bits that you saw the first time, are enhanced or reduced. Again watch it again all the way to the end and observe without judgement your experience. When you get to the end, watch it again for the third time, but this time enhance the positive experiences. The negative past experiences cannot be changed as they are in the past, but you can in this moment choose to release those by imagining your story in a much more positive light.

Chapter 7

A Little Bit of Basic Psychology - Our Personal Iceberg and our Basic Needs explained

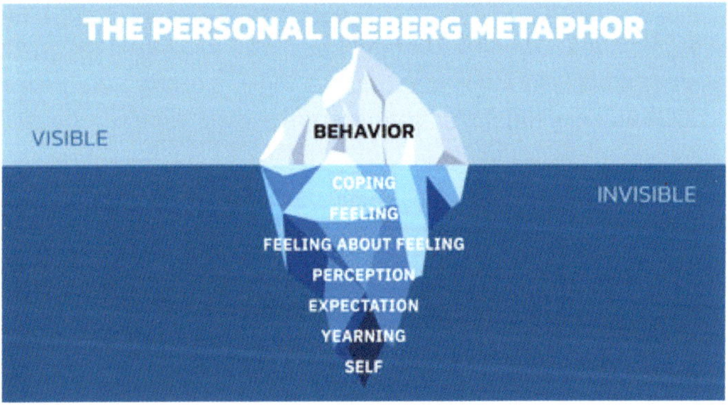

The idea of this model originates with Sigmund Freuds' model of Consciousness, where the tip of the Iceberg represents just 10 percent of psyche. On the surface we take in our information by what we see for example body language, behaviour, appearances, physical ailments and the environment.

We are taught negative thought patterns from a very early age:- from our parents, Don't touch that its dirty, don't jump of that wall, you'll fall and hurt yourself, from the teachers, Maths/ English/Sport etc is not your subject. Mates: Try this and you'll look cool etc. All of this information is subject to what we call limiting beliefs and are negative in connotation. If we are told it by someone we "look up to" then we believe it must be true.

The trouble is that our beliefs and values are taught to us by those who we trust implicitly. What we don't see however, is the thought processes, the emotions, the behaviour, the habits and the circumstances that lead to what we see outwardly. Everyone is on a journey and therefore it is important not to judge people on the language they use, the behaviour and appearances they exhibit etc.

It is possible however, to change limiting beliefs. How many people out there do you know who want to give up a bad habit? By changing their thought process, and the emotional attachment they have to that thought, we can change the pattern of behaviour that becomes a habit through circumstance, therefore changing the original belief and value they had around that habit. It can be changed by understanding how the brain functions, and doing some simple exercises shown. It's effectively like changing a programme that you don't want to watch anymore on the TV channel.

Maslow believed that for a person to be motivated to achieve great things, they must achieve certain needs. Those needs being listed below in a hierarchy achieved in turn. He believed that the longer a person goes without that need the more the desire. For example, the longer someone goes without food, the hungrier they become.

1. Physiological:- Food, water, breath, sleep, excretion.
2. Safety:- Safety in body, in mind, in soul, in health, employment and resources
3. Esteem:- Self esteem, confidence, respect of oneself and others and achievement
4. Self actualisation:- Creativity, spontaneity, acceptance, morality and the ability to problem solve.

What I never realised until fairly recently is that Maslow was much smarter that anyone truly understands. If you look at the image above of Maslow's Hierarchy of Needs, you can see the coloured image. The colours starting at the bottom are Red, followed by Orange, Yellow, Green, Blue. The colours of the rainbow. Which incidentally are also five of the seven colours of the Chakra system. Why is it important to bring this to your attention? Chakras are the wheel-like energy centres in our bodies that correspond to our emotional and physical well-being. Each one of these energy centres carries a piece of our identity including physical, emotional, ego, social, creative, archetype (self-reflection) and universal (self knowledge)

During covid, I brought together a team of integrated health professionals, including a doctor, a nurse, a pharmacist and different mental health professionals to discuss project rainbow. It was an interesting concept to me that the NHS used a rainbow as their logo during the Covid pandemic and being the inquisitive type, I wondered how integrating the colours of the rainbow would indeed help the pandemic as it unbelievably drew parallels to eastern medicine. Following a particular session with a key worker using colours to bypass the cognitive side of her brain, I realised how connected everything actually is. Confirming that with this project was my aim. Eastern medicine, western medicine, the body, the mind and the soul are all connected and if we had a system of integration our health and the system would hugely benefit. Helping us all to feel better, move more and sleep soundly.

The Red colour of the Chakra system, represents, grounding or roots. The adrenal medulla the inner part of the adrenal gland responsible for fight or flight is also situated here. (Root or base Chakra). It's purpose is survival, corresponding nicely with our physiological needs.

The Orange represents, the fear centre, connected to our metabolism, sexual organs and how we grow, this is known as the sacral chakra and if it's blocked can leave us feeling detached from our emotions, unsafe and insecure. It's purpose safety, sexuality and emotions.

Yellow represents our solar plexus chakra, situated in our gut just above the naval, which when blocked, can lead to low self worth, esteem and doubt with no sense of direction. You've heard the expression, gut feeling, gut, reaction or response but if this is blocked then our intuition is also affected. It's purpose is power and will.

Green connected to the heart chakra is all about love and the ability to both give and receive it. If this is unbalanced though, we can feel unworthy of love and this also can affect our self esteem and our relationships. It's possible that a blocked heart chakra can lead to a difficulty in accepting yourself, jealously or fear of being rejected. It's purpose is balance, love and relationships.

Blue is connected to the throat. If this is blocked you can struggle to express yourself, which in turn can lead to anxiety and insecurity, feeling afraid to speak your truth or fear of speaking in general. It's purpose is communication.

The Indigo chakra is connected to the third eye which is located at the centre of the head in between where the brows meet the bridge of the nose. This is also an EFT tapping point and is closely linked to insecurity, indecision, worry, overthinking and an inability to understand. It's purpose is clarity and intuition.

The violet crown chakra, situated at the top of the head, is opening up to be the best version of ourselves we can be and symbolic of all our wishes and desires. It's purpose is wisdom and knowledge (Self actualisation).

The chakras are the colour of the rainbow and when we feel balanced and not blocked, we are free to flow and the energy within us thanks us for that! Who doesn't want more energy?

Chapter 8

Food and its Challenges

Food issues are common place. They can be picky, fussy, faddy or all of the above or they can stop eating full stop. They can eat and throw up or take laxatives. Anorexia, Bulemia, Arfid, (avoidant restrictive food intake disorder), Binge Eating and Orthorexia are all on the rise but it's important to note that disordered eating patterns are not all about food. Often it's about feelings, control, a phobia or just the ability to cope. Trying to control life by denying yourself nourishment or having difficulty receiving love, using constant self criticism and pushing away problems instead of facing them, are some of the underlying subconscious emotions that underpin these disordered eating patterns. It's important to also acknowledge that our gut is linked to the brain axis which is hugely connected to our brain health with foggy brain, depression, anxiety, autism and schizophrenia linked to an imbalance in its flora. The gut itself is approximately six metres long and is the longest organ in the body linking top to bottom literally! If it's not fed and nurtured appropriately then the microbiome (friendly gut bacteria) that help to play a significant role in our mental and physical health will be depleted.

Self sabotage as this next case study proves, sadly will not help the problem disappear. Understanding and accepting the blocked emotion and releasing it, is a much safer way to feel better.

Self Image (Am I too Fat, too thin, too ugly,)

Lacking in Esteem (Belief that you are not good enough)

Memory Archive (Learned behaviour either conscious or sub-conscious) for example forced fed. Watched from the sidelines someone with food issues to include yoyo dieters.

Emotions/Grief/living in fight/flight - Feeling too sad, hurt or angry to eat, or feeling nauseous.

All of the above can contribute to negative eating patterns but please remember that it really is "too hard to be perfect!"

A very special brave person tells her story and sets out the techniques that helped her through the dark times. She's on a long journey and hopefully on the road to recovery.

My life was going great. Ironic as it sounds, I was studying Food and Nutrition at University and loving it. I had a fabulous boyfriend and had just been offered a fantastic placement for my year out. Life really did seem 100% perfect, to the outside world looking in.

Soon afterwards, the world, my four walls, my creation, came tumbling and crashing down around me. The word Anorexia hit me like a train crash. I knew I was thin, but I liked it. I loved the way I looked. I was in control and it really felt good for a while until I wasn't in control any longer. My energy was rock bottom, I couldn't function, I wanted to just sleep and crawl under a stone, my emotions were playing havoc with my life and I didn't understand any of it.

I embarked on this long long journey, to try and understand why? Why this was happening to me of all people, who loved food and who loved to cook. Why I was a feeder but couldn't face eating the delicious delicacies I conjured up.

No-one said it would be an easy journey and it wasn't. It was one of the hardest things I've been privileged to encounter. There were tears, there was anger and frustration, there was guilt by the ton, there was sadness and grief, but through it all I gained the trust of those who endeavoured to help me and came out the other side wiser and more aware. I'm still on my long journey and no one knows where to, but I'm hopeful with all the coping techniques, strategies and understanding I will end up in a much much happier place.

Emotions, play a huge part in how we stay stuck in the foundations of our subconscious world. This subconscious underground world is 88% more powerful ("Theory of Mind" Dr. Kappas), than our conscious mind which is only 12%. If we try and solve a problem with our conscious brain, that is stuck in the subconscious world, we will never succeed as we're looking in the wrong place. We will do everything in our power to survive but survival isn't necessarily a quality existence.

The remedy of any challenge will always be found in the root and therefore its important that we explore the complexities and systemic perspective of our brain. When we live beyond our limits, boundaries or capacity then our nervous system enters survival. Our experiences are then viewed from the lens of threat and as a result we deplete our internal resources. This shows up often as the emotions of anxiety, depression, sensitivity to criticism, resentment and a whole bunch of other stuff that we portray not just on our internal world, but also on the people around us. We must all create our own boundaries in order to learn to live within our capacity and remember everyone's capacity is different. It's too hard to be perfect.

Chapter 9

Emoticons and our Emotions

Which ones can you identify with? How do we process our emotions and what happens physically to us when we do?

Emotions are integrated by the Amygdala (the guard dog) and need to be processed to be released naturally. If they aren't processed naturally because they get stuck in a cog, then we feel the impact physically (Physical and Mental are connected!).

Physical versus Mental

We know that blood chemistry changes dependant on what is happening in your life. If we laugh it can heal us, if we're going through a particularly stressful time our immune system cannot do itself justice because it has to work twice as hard. We are intelligent beings otherwise our hair and eyelashes wouldn't keep replenishing themselves, our skin wouldn't heal itself after a cut and our hearts wouldn't beat. We know subconsciously how to survive, heal and grow.

This next story actually shows us, how connected we actually are.

I was suffering terribly with vertigo. The doctor had labelled it BPPV and gave me some exercises known as 'Brandt Daroff' to do at home.

I really struggled to do these basic exercises and my vertigo was getting worse, not better.

This made me doubt everyone and everything around me. I became a shadow of my self, with literally no confidence and I found myself giving up my life to just function.

What I never realised, was that my body was trapped in a loop of overwhelming and overloading emotions. It was stuck and I was going round and round in circles not knowing how to get off the roundabout I'd created for myself.

Anyone going round in circles on a roundabout would feel dizzy and eventually "fall off" or be sick and my body was communicating physically what was happening mentally in my internal world. I started to acknowledge each emotion I was feeling and as I did that I began to feel noticeably better. I knew at some level that the physical and mental were connected but never understood how that worked until I connected the dots ...... and everything became so overwhelmingly obvious that I'd been looking in the wrong place for the answer.

To release the physical feelings effectively, we need to understand the emotions we feel, just like the story above and also the example of anger that Eric (not his real name!) felt in the story below.

Emotions are just emotions and shouldn't be labelled good or bad. They can be painful though with a feeling that we want to run or push them away instinctively. If we allow ourselves to just sit with these feelings though without judgement or criticism, then it often provides us with a completely different experience and the emotion passes. Releasing them through colour and shapes is an interesting concept for those able to visualise. Again everyone is different and not all brains can visualise.

TASK

Close your eyes and notice the feeling. Where does the feeling start in your body and where does it finish? You may notice or sense it's in your head and extends down towards your heart or it may begin in your stomach and finish in your heart. Focus in on this area and then join the dots to get a shape. You may see a straight line, a triangle, a rectangle or square or a random irregular shape. Don't judge the shape, just be aware and notice it and then give it a colour. With a deep breath similar to a purposeful sigh of relief exhale the coloured shape outside of yourself and place it on a whiteboard in front of you. Observe the shape externally and then leaving that outside the body, go back inside and check in on the feeling, the shape and the colour. Has it changed? altered in size? Just notice with no judgement, just acceptance. Repeat until you feel an ease in the feeling.

Are we too frightened to show our emotions? Fear of being called a sissy, weirdo, baby, pull yourself together attitudes. What happens when we cry?

Eric was very angry, very angry indeed. He showed his aggression on a regular basis by punching anything from the walls to people injuring both property, himself and those that he was angry with.

Initially using this as a coping mechanism made him feel so much better, but he was left feeling guilty, selfish, confused and a whole array of other emotional overload that he then didn't quite know what to do with. None of it was his fault, he was just dealing with difficult situations that were too hard for his brain to process and he dealt with it, in a way that he thought was the best and only way, until he was shown a different route. A better route that led him to a much better and safer place.

This is his story and some of the techniques that he used to help him on is six week journey. If any of this resonates with you or anyone you know then please don't be afraid to seek assistance. There is always someone who will listen.

I was excessively angry. I was angry with life and with the people I really cared about. What I didn't understand was that every time I got angry, I also felt guilty. Guilty for upsetting my Mum, guilty for upsetting my Nan and Grandad, guilty for hating my brother. I'd punch holes in the walls of my bedroom to seek some relief. I'd scream and shout and end up just feeling sad and empty. No-one understood what I was feeling, no-one understood how or why. My behaviour to the outside world was not acceptable but internally I used it to fix my hurt. It helped in the short term but in the long term it caused me lots more hurt both emotionally and physically including a broken arm!! I knew I had to change but I didn't know where to begin and the people I cared most about didn't know how to help me either.What I didn't understand was how my brain functioned and why it kept creating, habit forming negative self help.

Once I changed the negative habits and my beliefs around them and released all the blocked emotional overload, stuck in my subconscious world, I felt lighter, like a big heavy weight had been lifted away from me, quickly followed by a sense of freedom. Emotional Freedom Technique is a hands on energy therapy technique that can be used to release anger, efficiently and effectively and there is definitely no need for a broken arm!! If everyone was taught this in schools, pupils would generally feel calmer and so would the teachers!!.

Changing my beliefs and looking at my personal values also helped me to shift my anger engaging in much healthier alternatives to get my endorphins, serotonin, oxytocin and dopamine fix.These are happy chemicals if you're wondering. These hormones and chemicals help with positive adrenaline which is the opposite of my anger which was depleting these happy chemicals and using my adrenaline in the negative.

I went to a boxing gym to help to alleviate some of my frustrations. Exercise is just one thing that can help activate all the happiness chemicals - so its a win win.The list below may be useful in understanding the different hormones.

Dopamine helps us to feel motivated to learn and for pleasure. It helps with will and determination to achieve our needs, wants and desires. Endorphins help to release happiness and can mask physical pain as its response to pain and stress causing anxiety, Serotonin helps us to accept ourselves and the people around us without judgement and Oxytocin helps us to feel loved and plays a role in bonding.

If we are deficient in Dopamine for example, we may have low self esteem, lack motivation, feel anxious, have low energy or fatigue. The good news however, is we can increase it by exercising regularly, creating something like writing or drawing or listening to music, we can meditate and we can eat foods containing L-Tyrosine, which include cheese, nuts, eggs, chicken and fish.

If we are deficient in Oxytocin, then we may feel stressed and lonely, we may disconnect from our relationships and may struggle with insomnia. Massage, physical touch, listening to music and exercise, being more sociable and meditating can all help.

Deficiency in serotonin can lead us to feel overly sensitive, be moody, struggle to sleep and have a compulsion, obsession or social phobia leading to anxiety and panic attacks and often at the root is low self esteem. Exercising, massage, sunshine or light, cold showers and exercise can all help to increase our happiness levels.

Endorphin deficiency can lead to aches and pains, mood swings, depression and anxiety and impulsive behaviour but laughing and crying, eating dark chocolate and spices, exercising, stretching (yoga) and meditating can all help.

Crying is definitely positive as it releases all these positive endorphins, which is why we feel better when we've had a good cry! Tears contain an analgesic (pain killer) property, which help to combat pain, so any tears sparked by emotion contain higher protein levels and play an important part in balancing our stress levels. Never be embarrassed to cry!

Chapter 10

Who or What is Perfect? - Body Image, Self Esteem and Building Confidence

What is perfect? I can guarantee if we ask a room full of people what they think perfect is we will get a whole host of different answers. Some will give answers around being kind, respectful, having no problems; some will give responses with materialistic undertones, to be very successful with lots of money with no financial worries etc etc. But the problem with perfect is that it's all about perception and someone's perception of being perfect is very different from the next. We live in a constant illusion.

Are we human beings? Or human doings?

Have we created a world of human doings, instead of a world of human beings? Have we forgotten how to just be because we are forever running. Running on the treadmill of life with no stop button. Running away from who we are, frightened of connection to our emotional, physical and spiritual load.

Are we too reliant and needy on our external world. The doctors office, our health service, our government and on it goes to fix everything in our internal world. I believe that it is only knowledge and looking at a full picture that can help us to fix ourselves. It's the full picture that is a little illusive to us all. We are only ever privy to a small window of the real story.

We live in a world of two halves the difference between night and day, black and white, stability and uncertainty. We want to be loyal yet we feel so much injustice.

We need to be straight talking to enable us to make any significant changes especially now, as we live in an upside down world. What if, we're looking in the wrong place.

Sadly we're all living in two spaces contradicting everything that we as human beings stand for yet we're living in a human doing world.

Whether that's target driven, materialistic, ego centric or power crazed. Whether we need to tick boxes or trying to navigate our way around bureaucracy - it's centred around the need to do.... What if we changed this to the need to be...... it changes the whole perspective.

We've hardened our internal spirit dulling it's light because of belief systems that don't even necessarily belong to us or the need to control everything that probably isn't within our power to control even though we may think it is. It's a myth that we think we can control anything other than ourselves and our own reactions and responses. We can't control anything or anybody else.

Expressions are such and therefore need to be expressed not compressed. Yet we spend our precious time being compressed by everything we do, trying to emulate someone or something - the newest 'TikTok', instagram post, seeking gratification from the external instead of seeking out our own internal light.

It's too hard to be perfect but we are perfect with our own imperfections. It's the imperfections that make us shine our light. It's never been about external perceptions or what we perceive to be reality. It's always been about our internal underground system that helps us every single day to see, to hear, to love and to touch, to feel and to sense, to breathe, to fight, to survive and to thrive. Have these abilities got lost?

It would always be too hard to be perfect if we look in the wrong place. Find your motivation, desire and passion to understand what's perfect for you and shine your light brightly.

I was always looking in the wrong place, seeking external worth. I never believed I was good enough especially after a lovely English teacher told me I was thick and stupid and would amount to nothing after hurling my work into a classroom full of young students.

Imagine carrying that belief around which then stuck in my cogs for years. I always wanted to be a teacher even when I was little - yet that statement knocked me off course for the best part of 20 years ....

Don't let someone else's belief system cloud your internal light. It's usually just a mirrored belief from their own frustrations which is a concept I learned many years later.....

I learned that it's ok to be imperfect - it's that imperfection that makes us unique and perfect just the way we are....

To live is the rarest thing in the world, most people just exist." - Oscar Wilde.

Please find your way to live in peace.

This is the story told by a beautiful girl who puts enormous amounts of pressure on herself to reach her impossible target of being 100% perfect. Yet she's not really sure what 100% perfect is as she's always moving the goal posts.

I'm a 19 year old student with exceptionally high expectations. I never realised they were so high but trying and then failing to be 100% perfect all the time, was truly exhausting, to a point where I crashed. I was scared and fearful about what was happening to me. I felt lost, alone and disappointed in myself. I was always studying hard but when I never achieved 100% or close to it, I felt sad and guilty. I spent so much of my time trying to build up my worth, based on an external body image that I perceived was perfect. I also spent many hours on my make up, hair and general appearance. Recently, I started to add Botox and fillers into that routine and it was costing me a fortune and yet I still didn't like what I saw. I thought it would make me happier but underneath my mask, I never truly felt seen, valued or heard and was struggling to thrive without feeling supported or validated. I was burnt out and I was never truly going to achieve what I needed to, without understanding that I needed to find an inner sense of belonging to understand who I was. The root of where these high expectations began and why I felt this urge to be perfect.

My mum also strove for perfection and when something didn't quite meet her expectations, she'd get agitated and stressed. I wonder where I learnt that trait!! Her Dad too, my grandad was always seeking out perfectionism. I never saw the pattern, until it was pointed out. It was a light bulb moment when realisation kicked in. I'm slowly starting to piece the jigsaw together and beginning to love and accept myself for who I am without my mask. Looking from the inside out, rather than the outside in has truly helped me to feel grateful and surprisingly much more confident than ever!

Burnout or sacrifice syndrome as well as imposter syndrome are common place in all who run on the treadmill of life, or whom twist themselves in knots to find that 'perfect' successful version of themselves. We can feel like something is wrong with us where shame, loneliness and anxiety or depression can manifest. It affects our sleeping patterns, our eating patterns and it can lead to severe stress and panic attacks. Not nice and very frightening when the physical symptoms include:- Heart pounding, panic or pain, tense or tight muscles, boiling hot or freezing cold, feeling nauseous, not eating at all, high blood pressure and even shortness of breath. The true healing is to fully accept and love that authentic version of self so it becomes stronger than the masked version, we created to survive. Always show up to life and be present. Pay attention to what has heart meaning and speak your truth about what matters most.

Chapter 11
Grief and Trauma

Unfortunately grief is part and parcel of life. It's really difficult to express how we feel at sad and difficult times and processing the emotions that follow can be challenging. This chapter will hopefully help each and everyone who is suffering with the grieving process.

What is the grieving process?

Elizabeth Kubler-Ross a famous Swiss American Psychiatrist and a pioneer in near-death studies spoke about the grief process as a curve. She developed the curve whilst working with personal change in grief and bereavement.

Everyone will go through the emotions along this curve which include shock, hurt, denial, bargaining, questioning and anger but not necessarily incorporate all of these emotions in the same order or at the same time. Some will deny that it's happened, some will be angry, some questioning and some feeling just uncontrollably sad. Some will feel all of these.

Grief comes in all shapes and sizes and for all manner of reasons. Essentially it's a huge emotional change or shift and it's important to embrace it not avoid it. The loss of someone or something special including pets, change of job, loss of an old life I.e parental separation or divorce, change in financial situations are all reason enough to grieve and sensitivity to other people's feelings and thoughts must be taken into account and processed accordingly.

There are many books specifically around grief for teenagers and young adults but I think this next story written by a beautiful young girl really resonates with what grief is all about and its emotions are personal to each and everyone who is grieving.

A 13 year old girl very sadly lost her pet dog Dandy. She was totally inconsolable even after her dad bought her a new one. This young girl didn't want a new one. She'd lost her best friend, her confidant, she felt that her life was falling apart and was very lonely.

She really hopes that by telling her story, it helps each and everyone who is suffering. She knows how it feels.

The only person that truly understood me was Dandy. He was my life, we did everything together, so when he passed away I was lost and very sad. Everyone tried to console me, but they couldn't because they couldn't really empathise with the feelings that were mine. Some of my friends said "Its only a dog, imagine if it was a family member" which made matters worse. I didn't want another replacement I wanted Dandy and he was my family. The sadness sat in my tummy and I didn't want to eat. It sat in my heart and could hear it pounding. I couldn't focus on my school work all I could think about was where Dandy was. I didn't really understand how I could feel better until I saw Jane, who explained the feelings and emotions I was experiencing in real time and how to sit and accept them. She helped me to understand that pushing them away or ignoring them would make them seem bigger and that wouldn't help them to shift. She taught me about the natural stages of grief and how everyone goes through these stages, which help to put it more into context and eventually I learnt acceptance. Dandy is always with me, wherever I go and the memories of our time together remain in my heart always.

A beautiful lady came to see me. She'd been through lots of consecutive losses and shock throughout her life and therefore subconsciously had created a metaphorical heart wall to protect herself from further hurt, harm or danger. Understanding a heart wall can be found in Chapter 12. The emotion around her heart was so strong she could actually feel her heart pulsating with sadness. Working with the grief and loss she felt, in metaphorical colours and shapes enabled her to release the feeling around her heart, so she felt so much calmer and hence better in herself.

Table of Grief.

In 1969, Elisabeth Kübler-Ross described five common stages of grief, popularly referred to as DABDA. They include: Denial, Anger, Bargaining, Depression and Acceptance.

TRAUMA

Trauma is a response to a disturbing or distressing life event which can overwhelm our ability to cope. It is a persons response and reaction to that life event that causes a whole range of emotional overload including feelings of a diminished sense of self, helplessness, hopelessness, pain, guilt, shame and loss. If one or a number of those feelings get stuck in the wheels or cogs of our system then they will stop us in our tracks.

Many thousands of individuals across the globe in their lifetime will experience some form of trauma yet often it isn't reported. Many hide that trauma and often through no fault of their own.

The impact that trauma has on society in general is huge with adverse childhood experiences having a notably greater indicator of risk. Any adverse experience has a profound effect on our metabolism, autoimmune function, obesity rates, drug and alcohol abuse, suicide rates, domestic violence and criminal behaviour. That's not to say that those children experiencing adverse childhood experiences will all end up with a poor outcome.

Recently there have been many incidents of reported trauma. The MEN Arena, Borough Market and London Bridge attacks and the Grenfell Tower fire. The on-going war in Ukraine. Knife and gun violence.

Victims of trauma suffer immeasurably often with post traumatic stress disorder and that life event will stay with them forever stored in the memory. Trauma affects all four of our different types of memory both explicit and implicit. Our explicit memory contains both semantic memory, the memory of general knowledge and facts and also our episodic memory, the memory of who, what and where of an autobiographical event or experience. Our implicit memory contains our emotional memory and the feelings that we feel during that experience and our procedural memory, the ability to perform a common task on auto-pilot. If we can release the implicit emotional memory that got stuck, after the emotional event then it enables the victims to move forward and potentially with post traumatic growth. Positive change resulting from trauma can play a hugely transformational role.

Cognitive psychological first aid, (a first aid technique used within 72 hours of the event helping to halt long term PTSD), Somatic therapy, (using sensation in real time), energy based techniques and yoga, work best for shifting the blocked emotions following trauma. Talking therapies can't help to release the blockages especially if they're stuck and frozen behind the heart wall and CBT can trigger further traumatic episodes and shouldn't in my humble opinion be used.

Movement of any description helps to release trauma because just like any other muscle that we exercise, the vagus nerve can be exercised and therefore stimulated to release emotional overload. That's why we alway feel better when we've been to the gym. Yoga, Tai chi and Qi gong are especially beneficial for vagal toning enabling our fight or flight response to calm.

The benefits of yoga and movement

Simple yoga sequencing using breath, with simple movement can be accomplished by anyone and can even be done in a chair for those that are less able. I believe that movement and yoga specifically, should be accessible to all. For those who struggle, or find it difficult to bend or to sit on the floor, this sequence helps to build confidence so that the mind and body flow as one. Movement is so important and helps to modify vibration, improve hormones, lower blood pressure, helps with circulation and balance and increases the blood flow to the brain for greater mind/body connection.

When we learn to breathe better, we live longer, as we calm the Amygdala (fight/flight) and the ANS system (Autonomic Nervous System).

Neuroscience research shows that the only way we can change the way we feel is by becoming aware of our inner experience and learning to befriend what is going inside ourselves." When we make the connection between the mind and body - magic happens. (Bessel A. Van Der Kolk, psychiatrist and author)

Achieving stabilisation of the autonomic nervous system (ANS) through yoga and breath can help people engage allowing them to begin to process trauma. Using this type of movement, clients can return to a baseline physiological state more quickly.

Yoga Sequence for trauma informed consideration

Breath work

Simple breathing exercises with extended exhales serves to integrate the mind and body system to take it out of fight and flight.

Qi gong

A few minutes of shaking the body, shoulders, arms, wrists and then the whole body can release any sense of anxiousness that sits within it.

Shoulder Roll and Rotating neck message

Shoulder rolls and rotating the neck releases tension that builds in the base of the neck. When we carry the world of worries on our shoulders that's where tension builds.

Side bends.

Bending sideways, can help with balance finding a healthier equilibrium.

Seated Twist

Twisting and rocking from side to side can help to integrate the left and right brain. As we twist with our hands on the side of the chair, gazing upwards, this helps to extend the spine which then helps to tone our vagus nerve.

Seated forward bend

Forward bends help to release tension in the back of the body, which is where we store fear.

Seated Cat/Cow to release back

Stretching out the spine and the back, helps to release stress in the fascia, helping it to unknot

Hip Rotation

Fear is stored in the pelvic region. Rotating the hips in a circular motion, left and then right, can help to release stored up fear.

Leg raises

Bending the leg 90 degrees from the floor, towards the chest, and then repeating on the alternate side as the weight shifts from one foot to the other. This is a lovely easy to help strengthen the core, which helps to build self esteem and confidence.

Rest and Relaxation

Integrating relaxation 'Nidra' style is just as important as movement.Visualisation can really help to integrate the mind and body connection. Colour healing helps to re-align and balance our chakras and can be done very successfully whilst sitting.

Begin by getting comfortable, placing the feet firmly on the ground.

Imagine a paint brush and a pot of paint. I want you to begin by painting the souls of the feet in bright red paint. Red is the colour of our roots and helps to ground us. It helps to promote energy, strength, motivation, confidence, will-power, courage, initiative and attention to detail.

Next paint the pelvic region in orange. Orange is the colour of safety, helping to stimulate the body and the mind, build self-esteem, optimism, inner-strength, creativity, self-expression, happiness and open-mindedness.

Next paint the gut yellow.Yellow is the colour of the sun. The sun brings with it heat, light and energy. See if you can imagine the sun's heat, light and warmth penetrating your gut as it heals. Notice.Yellow helps to uplift and cleanse. It gives us back self respect and confidence, self control and an ability to rationalise. It helps us to feel content and can build mental stimulation.

Follow with a green paint brush, painting across the chest towards the heart. Green is the colour of nature, that brings with it abundance, clarity, space, and life. Green promotes balance, harmony, self acceptance, renewal, and a compassion for oneself and others.

Coming upwards towards the throat and neck area, change the paint to the colour turquoise blue. Turquoise blue can be a-likened to the ocean in a remote island. Use the breath to make the sound of the ocean. Breathe in through the nose and then out through the nose restricting the back of the throat. The breath can then be heard from the ears, which actually sounds like the ocean. This helps to promote calmness within, cleansing, relaxation, healing and resilience.

Finally go upwards towards the top of the head and paint an imagined crown in violet. You are all kings, or queens of your own destiny. Violet helps to promote a sense of belonging, self respect and dignity. Elimination of past and anxiety provoking thoughts helps you to move on.

You are a now painted in the rainbow of colour. Feel the energy, sensations, feelings, movement within as you integrate the mind and body together helping it to ebb and flow through breath, movement and relaxation. Take a big inhale, followed by an exhale of relief (sigh of relief) as you begin to come back to this space but before you gently open your eyes, rub the hands vigorously together and notice what you feel. You may feel heat, warmth, light or friction but what you feel doesn't matter. Just notice and then place the hands on a part of the body that you believe needs to heal. Please don't think too deeply - just place them on the first part of the body that comes immediately to mind. Breathe. When you are ready rub your hands together again and this time place them over the eyes as you part the fingers to let in the light gently. When you are ready and taking your time. Open the eyes.

A beautiful thirteen year old was traumatised two years prior to coming to see me after being caught up in the MEN Arena attack. This is her story.

When I was eleven years old, I was in the Manchester Arena Attack at an Ariana Grande concert, with my mum and my sister. As a young girl I was traumatised and was also struggling to come to terms with what had happened. Even though my mum and sister were at exactly the same event, at the same time and saw exactly what I did, they seemed to process what happened in a completely different way to me and also from each other. I never really understood why that happened until memory was explained. Our memory banks had processed the information in a completely different way to mine and even though it had affected them, they didn't appear to experience the struggles that I was.

Two years after that attack, the panic attacks and anxiety just kept getting worse and consuming me. I was experiencing flashbacks and emotions from that night. Even small things, like listening to the radio, in case I heard an Ariana song and going shopping to large centres, made me feel overwhelmed. There were too many people there, exactly like there were at the Arena that night making me feel claustrophobic. Noise especially fireworks, triggered the painful emotions I felt back then, affecting my emotional memory. I also couldn't sleep.

After being taught about the brain, the vagus nerve and emotional freedom technique, I was able to release some of the stuck blocked emotional memory. I also used the TV exercise and it was interesting to see that what I remembered the first time around was different from the second and third time. Once I'd put a much more positive spin on the event, I noticed a huge shift in my behaviour and to my reactions to Ariana Grande's songs, loud noises and shock. I felt much more like me! After, I had released all the negative emotions my sleep pattern also returned to normal. Learning this has helped me to put everything back into perspective and to see it through a completely different lens.

Trauma for one is not necessarily trauma for someone else, but this lady suffered immeasurably at the hands of the people who were supposed to be her allies, her support. For the first time she has finally found her inner peace.

I was abused both physically and mentally by my parents. They didn't want a daughter only a son. Even the photographs on the mantelpiece depict the love for my brother and the sadness I felt, looking forlorn lonely and miserable. I never felt loved nor cared for.

No-one knew what was going on behind closed doors, however years later it became apparent that many did indeed know what was happening to me but chose the route of silence.

They were protecting themselves and didn't have the ability nor the courage to speak out or express what was happening to me. It was incredibly damaging to know that everyone knew, but sat in the background rather than do something to help me. That was just another layer of evidence for me to prove to myself that I wasn't enough. I felt invisible, was never included and punished myself in the belief that, that would help me.

Years of various types of talking therapy, beating myself up further with physical symptoms and emotional turmoil led me to the conclusion that cutting ties would be my best and only option.

Until recently, when I connected my dots, I never realised that my subconscious soul was holding on to a hidden protective heart wall protecting the emotions I'd frozen behind it. The emotions of love unreceived, abandonment, betrayal and worthlessness. Each of these emotions hiding behind the layer of the other. At the root was abandonment. It all made so much sense. I felt abandoned, yet by cutting the ties I was also doing the abandoning and those feelings of abandonment kept re-surfacing and triggering a reaction and a response from me. I wasn't listening to my soul and connecting the dots. I was looking for external validation rather than seeking internal validation. Deep down I knew I was worthy. Once I released the steadfast heart wall, using emotional freedom technique and belief coding, I felt a real sense of tingling throughout my body. I could feel the actual sensation of movement within. The energy that I had blocked within me was beginning to move and for the first time in my life I felt 'fixed". I'm so proud that I finally took responsibility for myself and looking forward to being the best version of myself I can be and that is just perfect enough.

This story is an example of power versus responsibility. Her parents and the people around her that knew what was happening, sadly used their power without taking any responsibility for their actions nor responsibility for her care or upbringing. She was however, their full responsibility but they chose and have continued to choose to ignore the ability to make things right. With power comes responsibility, with responsibility comes power!

Chapter 12
Addictions and Phobia's

Addiction is a psychological or physiological need for a habit forming substance or activity that becomes impossible to do without, and has become the main focus of attention to our detriment. When we can't have it, we experience extreme symptoms that can include physical, psychological or social effects.

The presence of cravings, the desperate need for something, loss of control of self or situation, compulsion for the substance or activity, and the consequences (positive or negative) are ultimately what causes us to feel the feelings of moods swings, internal conflict, anxiety, stress, pain and impulsivity. Human's will always look to seek for something externally (Survival) in the belief that we can eliminate the feelings or run away from the difficulties we may be facing. Recovery, however involves changing old patterns, unhelpful or out-dated belief systems and often lifestyles.

Emotional overload that often but not always underpins the anxiety and pain, includes anger, hurt, depression and stagnation. A feeling of a need to punish (self) in order to find a way out and pushing all these feelings in rather than finding a way to release and deal with them. It is a false belief and often a secondary gain (where the belief or the benefit of getting better doesn't out weigh the benefit of remaining stuck) that actually keeps us stuck in this viscous cycle of sadness, anxiety and pain. A secondary gain is generally an unconscious defence mechanism.

Vaping is really popular amongst teenagers but the addiction to them is also becoming very prevalent, with lots believing that nicotine isn't present. The love of the exciting flavours, the fact that everyone else is using them and a belief that they're a safe alternative to smoking doesn't help. Teens are much more susceptible to addictions whilst their brains are still developing.

This next story is a clear example of a teenage addiction to vaping.

After Covid, I was really worried and scared about going back to the real school environment. I was quiet and lacking in confidence and hiding behind screen learning suited me although I felt lonely and isolated a lot of the time. When I saw many of "the popular" kids vaping I thought I would give it a try in order to try to "fit in".

It helped me in the beginning or so I thought to feel better about myself, and whenever, I wasn't coping it became my comfort blanket. Initially, I believed it was helping me to focus, I liked the sweet taste and even the marketing made it appear teen friendly, but the cravings were becoming so frequent, I was fidgeting all the time and spent more time with it than without it. I never believed that it contained harmful stuff that could cause me an actual addiction.

Nobody tells you about the pitfalls and everyone around me was doing it too, so I thought it was safe. I never imagined that I was inhaling harmful chemicals and toxins that were actually dangerous for my brain and body.

I only realised it was a serious problem when I couldn't find my vape in the middle of the night when I woke up with a nightmare. I was shaking uncontrollably, my heart was racing, I couldn't breathe and was sweating. I thought I was actually having a heart attack. I never realised that this was a full blown panic attack until the paramedics arrived.

I had kept my "juuling" a secret as I knew my Dad would go mad if he knew. Now I had to tell them everything. I was so embarrassed. They were more supportive than angry with me but suggested therapy which I was reluctant to attend but thought it would be the only hope I would have in kicking this habit.

Therapy helped me to recover from being reliant on external relief that stemmed from my internal insecurities. It helped me to understand myself, build my confidence and self esteem and to look from the inside out.

This next story helps to explain the painful emotional baggage of an addiction.

I thought I had everything, an amazing family, supportive friends, and a cool job. Everything was going well until it wasn't. One social drink, led to another and another and before I knew it, I was consuming copious amounts of alcohol and eventually was confirmed as an alcoholic and despised myself and what had become of me.

I went to many talking therapy sessions, mainly because I was told to go rather than actually wanting help, only to feel like talking about it wasn't helping me. If anything it was making me feel worse getting totally frustrated and going round in viscous circles.

Alcohol was actually helping me cope, or so I believed (I was using it as a coping mechanism) with deep rooted feelings of sadness, loneliness, loss and abandonment. I felt like I was a waste of space and that I had no real purpose to continue, but alcohol distorted my perspective and part of me felt better for that drink. I was recommended to see Jane by a friend, who also sought help for an addiction and although I was exceptionally reluctant, I felt I owed it to my family to try one last time to get better. I was surprised at how quickly, week by week, the solution focussed therapy process was beginning to give me hope, something that I hadn't felt for years. Little by little, things started to improve one step at a time and it was the hope that helped me to continue on this much more positive path. I had been taking myself in the wrong direction and veering towards a very dangerous, uncomfortable and unsafe space. For the first time, I am now able to see some light, away from the dark place I was sat in and I have a plan going forward that includes loving and accepting myself without seeking perfection.

This client had built a heart wall that was so steadfast in secondary gain, effectively very stubborn it was difficult to get behind. Once he viewed his alcoholic self, through an imaginary mirror, we were able to then release the emotional wall and he was able to see everything with clarity.

Understanding a heart wall. What even is this wall?

When we go through difficult times, trauma, grief, change loss, or uncertainty, we separate a part of ourselves away from those feelings. In the story above, the client mentions, "part of him felt better for a drink" ! Many use that expression of part of me feels like this and the other part of me like that. It's almost like we're operating as two sides of the same coin. One half in heads and the other half in tails.

Imagine flipping yourself over permanently, one minute in heads and then the next in tails, no wonder exhaustion kicks in. We then end up going round in circles and may feel like you're actually lost. Expressions such as "I don't know who I am anymore" or "I'm all over the place" are common. Ultimately, the heart wall is there to protect us from further hurt, harm or danger irrespective of whether that's a real, imagined or perceived threat. It's a really smart thing to do, If you think about the heart as our main survival organ. The subconscious is going to do it's utmost to help it survive so it builds a protective layer (a metaphorical heart wall) and freezes the emotional load behind the layer so we don't have to continually feel that hurt.

Task

Sit for a minute and be mindful of a particular sensation you have within. Notice where it sits in your underground system. Does it sit in front or behind that wall? Don't judge it, just notice it with awareness and acceptance. Try characterising it. Maybe bring it to life and name it. Add some colour to it. The first colour that comes to your head. Don't think about it too deeply. Then notice what's happening to that physical sensation. Can you move it, or release it? Sometimes just by acknowledging and accepting something is there it can actually reduce our resistance to releasing it.

Phobia's

The Byzantine Emperor had an irrational fear of water believing he could possibly drown, when he saw an expanse of it. This was probably the first written recorded phobia in 600 B.C.E.

The Amygdala is considered to be the key player, in phobic behaviour patterns as it malfunctions with its associated brain structures.

As you read earlier in the chapter on neuropsychological education, the Amygdala is responsible for the fight, flight and freeze responses to fear. Once a person feels that fear the brain releases biological molecules that give us the physical and emotional symptoms of increased heart rate, blood pressure and accelerated breathing, amongst many other physical reactions.

Phobias can cause immense distress and panic attacks can often prevent us from functioning. They are more than a simple fear. Often this fear is consciously irrational but to the subconscious it makes perfect sense. If phobias are limiting your daily activities, interfering with school, relationships or work then please seek help. Cognitive behavioural therapy and clinical hypnotherapy can really help, as can many of the holistic energy healing approaches.

I've seen many such cases of phobia.

Common phobias include fear of:-

Snakes - Ophidiophobia

Spiders - Arachnophobia

Flying - pteromerhanophobia

Water - Aquaphobia

Sickness - Emetaphobia

Needles - Trypanophobia

Heights - Acrophobia

Closed Spaces-Claustrophobia

Dentist - Dentophobia

Fear of public speaking - Glossophobia.

The fear of open or crowded spaces. ... Agoraphobia

Some of the phobia's above can be avoided in everyday life. For example, you are unlikely to come across snakes walking to work and therefore avoiding one is relatively easy. At some point in life though we will have to come across needles for example, so if a phobia is present it would be wise to seek support in releasing it.

Two stories that really have stood out in my mind and related to intense phobic reactions are written beautifully below.

I was misdiagnosed with an eating disorder even though I was desperate to put on weight.

I was told this could only be managed, never cured and yet in a few weeks, I feel so much better and almost back to my normal self.

I was diagnosed with emetaphobia (intense fear of vomit) which started from a sickness bug in primary school which was going round. I saw many children be sick and I was so scared I would catch it even though I didn't!.

In my first year of high school, a boy was sick in the classroom and I had a really intense panic attack, which triggered my anxiety again. I couldn't stop myself from shaking and I couldn't breathe. All I wanted to do was get out and escape, but I couldn't. I had no idea what was happening. I became so afraid I started to reduce my food each day, not even consciously to begin with. I was terrified of being sick, and linked being sick with being full and was therefore also terrified of being full. I had constant stomach aches from severe anxiety and I thought it was because eating too much had caused it, which is why I kept reducing. Of course it wasn't actually fullness, it was anxiety and it had an incredibly tight grasp of me. I had no idea it was anxiety as nobody had explained it to me. I felt so trapped. Ultimately I was scared of my own body and there was no way of escaping it. You have to eat to stay alive! My brain also became starved so I couldn't rationalise, or even think straight. I had then lost so much weight, I had to be hospitalised. Eating only 500 calories a day, it was such a relief that I could see this would finally come to an end. Little did I know how traumatising hospital would be. I was tube fed, 200 calorie increases daily until I was having what met my 'nutritional needs'. Each meal I would have a panic attack, screaming and begging everyone to stop as I was absolutely convinced I was going to be sick. I was so shocked how everyone just ignored me and carried on, despite me being in so much emotional pain. My family would have to hold me down as I was being tube fed and sometimes grab my hands as I was trying to pull out my tube. I would do anything. Every day got harder, another 200 calories. If I felt sick today, then surely I would feel more sick by eating more the next day? After the longest, hardest month of my life, I was finally discharged. CBT was going to start. The sessions were tough, but I tried hard each session, desperate to get better. But nothing made any sense. I was being treated for an eating disorder when I didn't have one. I was being taught methods to cope but I couldn't use them as I would go into a freeze before any meal or snack. My anxiety just got worse and although I was now eating, mentally I was in the same headspace. I kept trying so hard, for what seemed like so long. Having panic attacks 5 times a day is not fun, and in between meals, I'd still be thinking about it. Feeling full and feeling sick. The worst thing in the world. After a while, it got too difficult. I started reducing again, my only way of coping. I'd lost all the weight I'd gained in hospital and was so close to being admitted once again. I was so lucky I wasn't, and thankfully, my mum had contacted Jane, as she couldn't see me suffer any longer. Immediately, I felt a bit of hope for the first time in so so long. Finally someone who understood, who listened, and someone who actually cared. All we both wanted was for me to get better, as quickly as possible! It almost seemed unreal. Jane was so uplifting and positive, I actually believed I would get better again. At the beginning, I found it quite hard to talk about my feelings as I was shy and most of it could feel quite painful. So I'd email a few days after each session, updating her on my thoughts and feelings and what we could work on next. I found this much easier as it can be quite hard to think on the spot in the sessions. The therapy was really flexible and was bespoke to my personal needs and brain pattern. We used lots of visualisation and hypnosis techniques which helped me the most, as I am visual learner. I had lots of shifts along the way until eventually I realised I was pretty much better! I could go back now and then if little things came up, which I did. And now it's just more about challenging myself and jumping hurdles, knowing even if I am anxious, I can cope just fine. I connected the dots looking from the inside out and I'm inspired to now help other people with traumas and phobias as I know how debilitating they can be.

The next story shows how the subconscious can really grasp onto a phobic response, despite consciously having no recollection of the root cause.

A client came to see me as he was absolutely terrified of cats. He was so scared that if he saw one, he would sprint away not caring if that endangered his life. On one such occasion, he ran into the path of an oncoming vehicle and nearly got killed. Consciously he knew this was totally irrational, after all, what harm could a harmless cat do to him, yet he was terrified enough to have this intense phobic reaction of sweating profusely, fast beating heart and feeling utterly sick. His best mate had just got a cat for Christmas and he was too embarrassed to tell him that he was scared, so avoided the situation and just stopped going to visit. This angered his friend and tortured him because neither had communicated the other's perspective. One thought he'd done something wrong and the other was too embarrassed to explain the reasoning behind why he had stopped visiting.

The root cause was found after a clinical hypnotherapy session.

Here is his story.

When I was a tiny baby I was left outside a small newsagents shop in a leafy green suburb in my pram, whilst my mum had nipped into buy a newspaper. She was only gone less than five minutes but when she came out, she found me crying uncontrollably and noticed a big scratch on the side of my little cheek. She looked around but could see nothing and so had no idea what had happened but like any mum consoled me by picking me up and hugging me. I calmed down and the incident forgotten. Mum never left me unsupervised in my pram ever again!

Years later, I went to seek some help after my best friend got a cat for Christmas. I was so scared that I avoided visiting him. Consciously, I knew that this was a totally irrational fear, after all what could a defenceless cat do to me, but it was easier to avoid my friend than tell him I was scared of his cat. What I didn't know was that my subconscious had remembered this event very clearly even though my conscious brain hadn't remembered it to logically file it away. It turned out that a cat had inquisitively leapt into my pram whilst I slept peacefully and scratched my little face. No wonder my subconscious had written the story of fear of cats and had humiliated me even as a baby. What I also didn't realise was that I had mirrored the "scaredy cat" phrase and that's what had stopped me expressing my feelings and emotions to my friend for fear of humiliation. Once I'd connected the dots, had this episode confirmed by my mum who had also forgotten about it and communicated all of this to my friend, I was free to file it away in my logical brain and no longer had any fear of cats. I even picked up "snuggle" who was very cute and like velvet to touch.

Chapter 13
A little bit about colour

Life contrary to how we see it, is not really as black and white as we believe. It is full of beautiful shapes, images and colour, woven into each and every unique aspect of our very being and into the external world we see. Flowers, animals, paintings, our food, the sea, the land, the moon and the sun all depict some form of colour. Fashion, magazines, books, wallpapers, soft furnishings all allow us to be as creative as we like. Colour psychology has been used for years to create that beauty and to enable us to feel better - alive.

Life would be quite dull and boring if everything was indeed black and white. Wearing clothes that are colourful can make us feel better, more vibrant. I was working with a lady who was struggling to express herself. She couldn't really speak up for herself. I asked her to place a blue scarf around her neck and then to observe what happened. To her amazement that simple task helped her immensely. Spending time outdoors really helps us all to feel better. Have you ever wondered that maybe it's the connection to colour that helps us to feel more alive. When we paint a room, we can feel the difference in many ways. We can get the affect of calm by painting a room in a soft accent of aqua. If we go into a dark and dingy space, we may find ourselves feeling a little sad or even unsafe. Wearing gold can give us the feeling of abundance and white can help to lighten us up.

Years later I discovered, how accurate colour actually is and now I use it to release blocked emotional overload without the need to bring that emotion to the surface. Colour truly is a gift. I am truly amazed, grateful and sometimes mind blown by how quickly and painlessly release happens:- Red can be used to heal, depression, negativity and shyness, Orange can be used to help trauma, stress, bereavement and loss, gold can be used to treat stress and anxiety. Yellow can be used in the healing of despair, fatigue negativity, sensitivity to criticism and confidence, Green to help with anxiety, confusion and self pity. Turquoise to release anger, stress and anxiety and blue to help calm insomnia, stress, anxiety, excess adrenaline and anger. Indigo to release anger and obsession, violet to help with low self esteem, and obsession, Magenta to release aggression and pink for resolution for difficult relationships, anger, aggression and over sensitivity. Again look at how the dots connect together in all aspects of psychology.

I have recently been working with a young girl who found herself feeling very moody and sad. She always wore black and believed herself to be both fat and disgusting. She was retreating from her very own self. She was neither fat nor disgusting. She wore a dress size 10 and was very pretty. She was looking through a distorted lens. I got her to draw the dots of where the mood and sadness started and finished and the three shapes and colours she pulled out was a black circle, a pink square and a yellow rectangle. The black circle was indicative of her going round in circles to protect herself, giving herself strength and retreating. The pink square was about trying to find internal unconditional love and the yellow rectangle was a block that she'd put into her subconscious programme about purification. She hated herself, she put so much pressure on herself to be perfect and it had manifested in moods and sadness. She was looking at the wrong programme believing she could fix the subconscious with conscious thought. She thought restricting food would help her stay slim but that just knocked her metabolism off limits hence the moody and sad behaviour. Her vagus nerve had been completely destabilised and once we put it back in its place and changed the belief system, so she could see it from a wide angled lens, she felt brighter, lighter, calmer and more relaxed.

TASK

If you feel all over the place and not grounded, try imagining double sided sticky tape underneath the souls of your feet as you place them on the floor. Imagine roots growing down from underneath them and then progressively notice each and every single body part, starting with your feet, ankles, calves etc squeezing and releasing each part as you go. By the time you get to your face, neck and head you should feel much more stable.

Then use the rest and relaxation exercise above in the yoga and movement section to paint yourself as a rainbow. Colour definitely helps.

Are you beginning to connect the dots, the pieces of the jigsaw?..........

Chapter 14
Life and it's drama

Life is full of drama! Let's face it most thrive on a bit of gossip especially if it's about someone else's life. Do we play the parts of victim, persecutor and rescuer living within our very own drama triangles? (Steven Karpman)

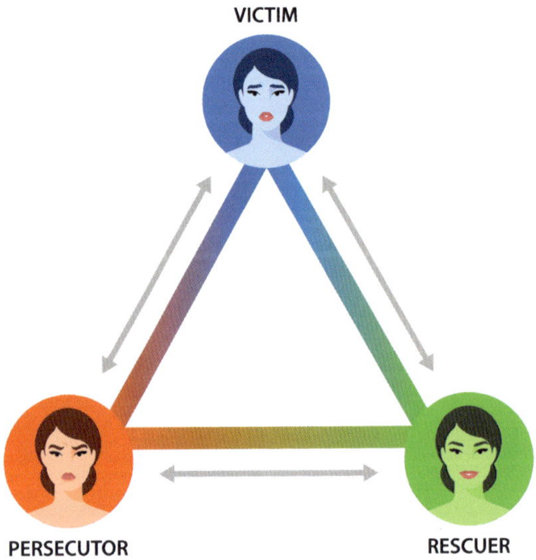

Human behaviour is drawn to that drama, even its about creating self drama or finding drama within our relationships or friendship circles.

We really don't have to look very far to prove that point. TV series are dramatised, so that millions of viewers tune in. The media, social or otherwise create drama storms to sell their stories and TV shows like Big Brother, Love Island and I'm a Celebrity all heighten the drama cause.

People come in numerous varieties, shapes and sizes, with a myriad of complex life stories. That's what makes us interesting and forms the canvas of human life but what works for some really doesn't work for others.

We will always find ourselves gravitating towards personalities that are or have similarities to our own.

Subconsciously, we are drawn to connection and often seek to complete a void within. If we're caring, we'll always find a way to help, if we're vulnerable, we'll find a way to find inner strength even if we have to borrow those benefits from somebody else. If we dramatise someone else's life, we don't have to think about our own. Remember my English teacher that threw my essay across a classroom of 13 year olds declaring "you're thick and stupid and will amount to nothing"!! Creating all that heightened drama!

What I didn't understand until years later was the fact that she was mirroring how she felt within (inadequate) as she was unable to express what the rules of the essay writing she required was, in language that was understood by all. Remember those representational systems! I was looking through a completely different lens and had understood the requirements incorrectly in her eyes. I made a mistake, I wasn't perfect. Her inadequacy as a teacher was mirrored clearly and on display for a whole classroom to witness.

Foundations of the human psyche is based on strong communication, trust, integrity, intuition and personal values. If emotional drama enters, toxicity (poison) grows and destabilises the very gut brain axis that causes internal inflammation. The vagus nerve then wanders into the stress response, believing or perceiving that we're not safe.

When drama plays out in character parts and we aren't aware or can't see that bigger picture or someone is hiding behind deceit then our identity is ultimately being questioned. Who are we and why are we playing that part?

Getting to know and understand people with all layers is a skill because we all have complicated layers of experience, history, emotional overload, family values and tradition.

True and genuine friendships, relationships and partnerships, only last the course if all the layers are loved and accepted. The most important part though is self - the core soul of our very being. If we don't love and accept that part, we get lost, feel unsafe and the drama settles and gets stuck or gets passed on down the generations. Hard to believe but we know that we get our DNA hair colour, body shape etc from our parents, science has now also proven that we also inherit emotional DNA.

Drama, judgement and bias, whether that be conditional or unconditional throws different perspectives and meaning into the canvas of our lives. Understanding how that plays out, I think is clearly expressed in the following stories.

I was with someone, who I really truly loved. He was a true charmer, charismatic, had a fantastic sense of humour and seemed to make light of the mundane parts of life. I loved those qualities in him until I found out that he had a completely different persona hiding in his underground system. A devious, manipulative and clearly troubled character was soon revealed. Little things didn't make any sense and part of me didn't want to believe what the other part of me knew deep within. My intuition was 100 percent accurate, but the other part of me thought I was going mad!! I had no idea that two halves of the same person were polar opposites and I found myself living with a true narcissist. One last straw, professional help, a supportive family and friend network and lots of strength, I finally set myself free but I needed to understand for myself a view from the wider lens.

I was living within an acute psychological drama triangle (Steven Karpman). I was a victim, even though I couldn't see that at first, I stayed in that loop perpetrating my own victim hood believing myself to be "mad" and not trusting my instincts and then rescuing myself with a metaphorical life jacket and using him to float! Part of him used my life jacket which for a long time helped him to stay buoyant.

I didn't understand until now that his picture had never been completed and it was my buoyant life vest that gave him subconsciously what he needed. The void of a strong family, stability and friendship groups he was missing. His child like ID remained infantile in function and as an adoptee his ego felt crushed so he sought to look for the missing void and pieces he felt had been lost. His ego had been bruised and as a result started to seek out ways to boost his self esteem. He needed to find a way for his conscious to mediate between his unconscious to test out what he thought was his reality. He was externalising his drama instead of seeking to find the root of his internal drama. For a long time I was part of that drama!

Thankfully, I connected the dots enabling me to see everything from a wider lens which has helped me to finally move on:-

Chapter 15

A brief understanding of some of the different therapeutic techniques and how they are used to help.

There are many different therapeutic models and different types of therapy. Here is an basic overview of a selection of the ones that I use and a few of the different exercises that have helped many of my clients for you to try. If you need further support, please seek professional help.

Person-Centred therapy is a non-directive therapy where the therapist provides an empathetic and supportive environment for the client to explore their own feelings and experiences. The therapist does not give any advice or make any diagnosis. It's three main principles are those of positive regard, empathy and congruence to enable the client to make any necessary changes to grow.

Psychodynamic therapy focuses on the unconscious processes of past experiences that are influencing emotional load and behaviour in the present . Techniques to help the clients gain some knowledge of internal conflicts are used. Transferring one emotion to another is quite common, when trying to escape from pain but the load that sits underneath in the underground system will eventually explode and catch up. Sometimes it's helpful to look at the emerging patterns from the past to explore if these patterns are connected.

Transactional Analysis is looking at behaviour, social relationships and personality (the ID, Ego and Superego, chapter 4) to help us to understand the interchanging, critical and nurturing, intuitive and dependant aspects of early lives.

Neuro-Linguistic Programming

Neuro = Brain

Linguistic = Use of Language

and How we programme are brains through the use of language

Cognitive Behavioural Therapy -

This therapy helps clients to challenge their old belief patterns and negative thoughts that are restrictive or contributing to psychological issues. Understanding these patterns often helps the client to modify their thinking and behaviour.

Try the following exercises:-

Dividing exercise

Current Belief Exercise

Relaxation and Releasing Techniques

Breathing Exercise,

Body Scan

Balloon stress release

Mindfulness

EFT -

Emotional Freedom Technique, Why and how its used

Enclosed diagram of EFT Points

Inner Re-patterning is a mindfulness technique used to release layers of stuck belief and trauma to a state of inner peace and calm.

Gestalt Therapy - What is Gestalt therapy and how it is used

Time Line - Create a time line and discover a pattern

ACT Therapy (Acceptance and Commitment)

Personal Values

NLP.

QUESTIONNAIRE:-

EXERCISE TO WORK OUT WHAT DEFINES YOUR REPRESENTATIONAL SYSTEM

EXPLANATIONS OF WHAT THIS MEANS

VISUAL 40% population

KINAESTHETIC 40% population

AUDITORY 10% Population

AUDITORY DIGITAL 10% population

Take a few minutes to answer the following questions, but please do it spontaneously. Don't think about it too deeply.

4 = closest description to you,

3 = next best description of you,

2 = next best and

1 = least descriptive. Use only each number once.

1. My important decisions are based around:-

   My gut feelings

   If it sounds right,

   If it looks right

   If I study and review what is in front of me.

2. During a confrontation, I am most likely influenced by:-

   The other person's tone of voice

   Whether I can the see the other persons point of view

The logic of the argument

Whether I am in touch with the other persons true feelings.

3. I communicate what is happening internally by:-

   The way I look and dress

   My feelings

   My spoken words

   My voice tone

4. It's easiest for me to:-

   Find the ideal volume on a stereo system

   Find especially relevant points intellectually in interesting subject matter

   Find the most comfortable furniture

   Work with rich colour combinations

5. I am very tuned into the sounds of my surroundings

   I am very good at making sense of data and facts

   I am extremely sensitive to the way textures feel

   I respond to the way a colourful room looks

   Please complete and fill in the grid below to determine which is your preferred system. You may be surprised.

	V	A	K	AD
1				
2				
3				
4				
5				
TOTALS				

CBT Exercises

What is Cognitive Behavioural Therapy?

We all have different and unique patterns of thinking, feeling and behaving. The underlying problem, is that we see the world as we are and not as it is. The story we tell ourselves is ultimately is how we react and respond to our unique experience. (Have you done the exercise above on representational systems?). These patterns can affect us and our experiences, but altering or seeing these patterns from a different perspective can actually help to alter any stuck patterns of behaviour, that no longer help us. If we take a look at how our brains process information, we can then see how that processing affects the behaviour. Cognitive thinking can be changed, altered or modified, which in turn can lead to more desirable outcomes.

Try dividing yourselves into four quarters.

Thinking - How does a particular thought affect you

Feeling- What feelings show up, where are they in your body. (Head, neck, throat, heart, stomach etc. Just notice, without judgement or criticism and when you hold that space, notice what happens to the feeling. Does it intensify or get smaller. Breathe through it.

Sensing - What sensations do you notice when you hold the feeling. Is it uncomfortable? Are you using avoidance to help you cope?

Action- Try to think of how you may take action to reduce those feelings and thoughts. Is there a better way to cope. Breathing through this process, can help to reduce, the fight flight response as it re-balances the vagus nerve that runs between the brain and the gut, so it not longer imagines that it has to fight, fly or flee the situation.

BELIEFS

Stuck beliefs are often those beliefs that we have inherited from parents, peers and teachers. They don't necessarily belong to us. What do you truly believe and value?

TASK

Current Belief exercise

Get yourself some A4 Sheets of Card.

On each one mark down the following:-

1. CURRENT BELIEF
2. OPEN TO DOUBT
3. MUSEUM OF OLD BELIEFS
4. PREFERRED BELIEF - OPEN TO BELIEVE
5. CURRENT BELIEF

Stand on each card in turn answering the questions accordingly as you move through the sequence of cards

What is your current belief around this particular problem, where has it come from, how long have you had this belief and why did you develop it?

Can you think of any reason why you may start to now doubt that this current belief is real? Write down any of your doubts.

Imagine that you have a vessel which we are going to call your Museum. Place any old beliefs you now have into this vessel. Do you want to stay within that vessel? If not, lock it away, move it, put it on one side. It may help to close your eyes when you do this.

Look at your preferred belief now. Are you open to believe that this has altered or changed?

If you now look at the current belief that you started with, I bet it's changed or altered and sometimes this can shift the block.

Breathing Exercise

Breathing like this is the best way to stabilise the vagus nerve, to stop it from running away, fighting a particular sensation or freezing on the spot.

Find somewhere quiet, away from noise.

Take a deep breath all the way down to the belly button.

Breathe in for three counts, hold at the top for four counts and exhale as if you're blowing away a feather for five counts.

Breathe in for five counts and out for seven counts as if blowing away a feather. (No holding it at the top this time)

Breathe in through your nose for three counts and out through your nose for five counts. Restrict the back of the throat a little as you exhale through your nose and you may find you can hear the sound of the ocean in your ears. Listen carefully for that ocean sound and when you have it, close your eyes and pretend you are at the beach.

Repeat these three exercises, three times each. Notice what happens. Perhaps you feel calmer, more relaxed and maybe even your heart rate slows. The reason this happens is because of neuropsychology. Breathing sends a message to the part of the brain to say you are safe and you are not currently in danger!

When we are anxious we automatically breathe shallowly from the top of our chests. This then sends incorrect messages and signals and the hormone cortisol around our bodies, indicating to our brain that we are in fight, flight or freeze mode. Remember its all about Neuropsychology. If we continue to breath as if we are anxious the whole time, then are switch remains on and our guard dog is permanently barking.

Body Scan

Find a comfortable position and close your eyes.

When you are ready move your attention to your toes, be aware of any sensations, warmth or coldness or any tingling feelings. Next turn your attention to the ball, heel, sole, ankle and the sides of your feet. If its easier, do one foot before the other.

Move your attention, to your shin, calves, thighs as you scan each area individually. Notice your breath and how it rises and falls in rhythmic movement.

Follow the same procedure into your pelvis, lower abdomen and lower back and notice any emotions that live here.

Move your awareness now to your chest and upper back. Notice your lungs.

Next move to your throat, neck and then mouth. Notice the muscles in your jaw and notice the coldness and warmth of your ears and nose. Move to your eyes and blinking. Is there a difference between one eye or the other.

Spend a few minutes being aware of your body as a whole and feel complete, still and at peace.

If you experience any uncomfortable feelings try sitting with them with curiosity. Realise that they aren't permanent if you face them with kind friendly awareness.

Listening to a relaxation tape is always a great option if you feel out of sorts or stressed out. There are many app's that can help and often many of them are free.

Balloon Release Exercise

Imagine that you have many worries that are weighing you down or sitting on your shoulders making you feel tense or heavy.

Visualise a helium balloon in a colour of your choosing and one by one place that worry or concern in each of the coloured helium balloons. Make a note of the coloured balloons you chose and for what worry. Using chapter 13 (A little bit about colour) are you able to see the emotional bigger picture? Release those balloons by using an imagined pair of scissors to cut the ribbon or rope to which the helium balloon is connected and watch it fly and then disappear out of sight. Notice how you're feeling now.

Mindfulness

Understanding what it is to be mindful and how we can live in the present and not in the past or in the future.

Mindfulness is an amazing process that helps us to purposefully pay attention to the present. The experience and practice has been scientifically proven to make us feel calmer, more centred and actually improve our physical well-being.

TASK

Pick up an object. Take a really close look at it. If your attention moves away from the object, that's fine just gently bring it back. All I want you to do is to look very closely taking in everything you see. I don't want you to touch or move it and it's important that you don't judge it for utility or beauty.

Next, I want you to close your eyes and remaining still, be aware of any physical sensations, where you body touches your clothes and if you feel pressure from the floor or the chair.

What can you hear? Maybe your just hear your breath or maybe there are external sounds coming from outside or the office.

Ok, you can open your eyes. What was your experience?

By focussing solely on the objects and then on sensations and sound, your brain has had a complete rest from any pre-occupied thoughts.

It's all about living more in the moment and less in the past or in the future.

Emotional Freedom Technique

What is emotional freedom technique (tapping). Emotional Freedom technique is an energy technique that works on tapping specific acupressure points of the body. It's a bit like strumming a guitar to get sound, if we tap on the various different points of our acupressure system we get vibrational internal sound that helps to shift blockages from within the cogs.

I like to view the body like the London Underground Tube Map. We have main stations, similar to Euston, Waterloo and St Pancras with various different smaller stations reaching off those main stations. Our main stations work in-line with the Chakra system. We have one at the top of our head, one at the throat/neck, one in the heart, one in the stomach, one in the pelvic region and one in our feet. What happens if the trains going into Euston, St Pancras or Waterloo, get stuck, due to strikes or blockages on the line, then chaos ensues. Everyone is delayed. The same happens to us. If we get blockages on or in our lines, then chaos ensues and everything slows down and eventually gets so blocked up, there is no space to move, or has no where to go. Tapping or EFT helps to release those blockages, safely, quickly and effectively so our energy system inside feels relief.

During the EFT protocol, you are guided to tailor made wording targeting the specific problem whilst tapping on these specific acupressure points. We say things like "even though I feel ...... if it's anxiety you're feeling you would say anxious, if sad you would say sadness etc, I'm still going to love and accept myself. Loving and accepting self is the key in how energetic blockages shift. These therapies have been validated for efficacy and speed in resolution in many physical and psychological conditions and have been clinically trialled.

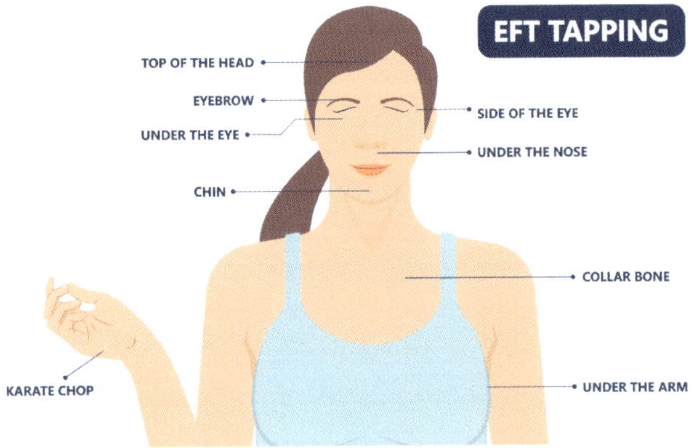

The diagram shows the Emotional Freedom Technique points but feel free to view the various different "you tube' videos. Seek professional help if needed. EFTi is the regulatory body that qualified EFT practitioners can be found.

Mindfulness Based Inner Re-patterning

This technique is based on the concepts of mindfulness, a state where we are very much focussed in the now and aware of our experiences and tapping. It's where we can be aware of a particular thought that pops up without actually thinking about it. Scientific research has found that using mindfulness techniques can reduce stress and anxiety. This particular technique can release layers of old stuck beliefs, emotional overload and re-frame distorted perception.

Gestalt Therapy

This therapy helps to centre on awareness, self direction and freedom and focuses on the present moment rather than any past experiences. It can be used to help anxiety and stress, tension and in part addictions. A therapist may ask what is happening "now" or where is your anxiety situated right now? It helps to improve self awareness and knowledge.

Time-Line Therapy

Time line therapy was developed by Tad James allowing clients to release negative emotions linked to something negative that happened in their past. Releasing the emotions and understanding the thoughts and behaviour that are connected can help.

The brain as I've said before is the most powerful computer in the world and most only use around 10 percent of its capacity. Imagine being able to use even just 20 percent. It only remembers really positive stuff and really negative stuff. It doesn't really remember incidentals like how often we visit a supermarket. It files those occasions away appropriately as its not really relevant to our daily life.

TASK

If we sit for a minute and just list from the year we were born, to present day a time line of events, we remember, both good and bad, often a pattern appears. Is that a positive pattern or a negative one? You may remember your first day at school, or family occasion like a wedding or a exciting family holiday. Or alternatively, you may remember a significant loss, being bullied or having an embarrassing moment, just like I did. Have a look at the pattern and see how that pattern has affected your belief system going forward. What behaviour you exhibited and what thought runs along side it.

I truly believed for years that I was "thick and stupid" and would amount to nothing and as a result, lost hope, had low self esteem and anxiety for years. I forgot about all the good and positive stuff I'd done and honed in specifically on that event. My belief system, rightly or wrongly got stuck and my brain found all the negative experiences it was looking for, hence the evidence. I was looking in the wrong place and so was my teacher!! Once this was released, my world opened up and my lens became full and wide-angled.

Acceptance and Commitment Therapy

Acceptance and Commitment therapy is a treatment that addresses the human need of happiness focussing on behaviour and how that determines the quality of our lives. Understanding that none of us are perfect, it teaches us to accept all our flaws and imperfections by gently steering the direction of our lives into a better space. It focusses on acceptance, defusing cognition to alter the way our thoughts affect us, being mindful. It teaches us to see ourselves from three different aspects of context, concept and process. with context being our sense of self, concept around deep rooted beliefs about who we actually are and process, which is all about us evolving from past to present and into the future. Personal values are another important part of ACT therapy in order that we can action commitment in our knowledge and skill set.

VALUES TASK

Below is a list of around 100 words representing different personal values:- Look at them carefully and highlight your top five in accordance to how important they are to you.

Acceptance, Accuracy, Achievement, Adventure, Attractiveness, Authority, Autonomy

Beauty

Caring, Challenge, Change, Comfort, Commitment, Community, Compassion, Contribution, Cooperation, Courtesy, Creativity

Dependability, Duty

Ecology, Excitement

Faithfulness, Fame, Family, Fitness, Flexibility, Fun

Generosity, Genuineness, God's Will, Growth

Health, Helpfulness, Honesty, Hope, Humility, Humour, Independence, Industry, Inner Peace, Intimacy

Justice

Leisure, Loved, Loving

Mastery, Mindfulness, Moderation, Monogamy

Non-conformity, Nurturance

Openness, Order

Passion, Pleasure, Popularity, Power, Purpose,

Rationality, Realism, Responsibility, Risk, Romance

Self Acceptance, Self Control, Self Esteem, Self Knowledge, Service, Sexuality, Simplicity, Solitude, Spirituality, Stability

Tolerance, Tradition, Trust

Virtue

Wealth, World Peace

Once you have five highlighted words. Connect the dots! If for example you have picked health as one of your top values and you aren't looking after it …… maybe you're smoking or vaping and its becoming a problem, or eating a poor diet, then that's what you need to improve….

Chapter 16
Concluding thoughts.

It appears that we are living in an ever changing world that seemingly plays out in a game of snakes and ladders. Many are suffering with the exhaustion of sliding down the slippery snake all too often. Many are trying to climb ladders that are unachievable aims.

If we take our lives and imagine for one minute that we are climbing this huge ladder to reach whatever goal we set for ourselves in a moment in time only to find soon after, that we're sliding back down our original pathway not dissimilar to the slippery snake and finding ourselves back at our starting point.

What if everyone is living in this game? Are we human beings with emotional energy in motion, needs and wants or are we just human doings? Copycatting off the back of someone or something. Trying to climb a ladder that we don't even know why we're trying to climb. A belief that we should live life this way or that way because that's how our families, friends, and ancestors lived.

Maybe we feel huge injustice, life is not fair?, how does that happen?, why?. Can we alter reality or perception? We need loyalty and leaders who can stand up to the realisation that human beings are not wired to do the things that human doings believe are possible. We don't take into account human behaviour, human emotion and our need for survival.

If we look closely, we see this play out in many scenarios. At the doctors, a one size fits all pill helps with every conceivable dis-ease, In the law courts, a law that doesn't take into account human beings and their emotions, behaviours and encountered personal traumatic experiences, backstabbing and bullying coming from a distorted Ego perspective. In schools, where children are boxed off even before they understand why they aren't in that set, or why they struggle to understand or read. Everything becomes lost in translation because of what is an illusion, perception of how we believe or perceive we should live, how we should be, how thin or how fat, how tall or how small, how clever or how thick. Life is not black and white, there are solutions to every problem and self care, nurturance, forgiveness and compassion go a long way to helping us to fight our lived experiences with love and gratitude.

I believe everyone has a place here on this earth to travel their own journey, through their own eyes, with no comparison or judgement. There is no one size fits all society but condoning behaviour that is only seen through one set of spectacles is looking at only a fraction of the much bigger story. ...... We must integrate all the pieces in order to see a much clearer vision and looking at connecting our mental and physical health is a great place to start.

Thank you's 🙏

There are many people I'd like to thank for their support in bringing my vision to life.

To my gorgeous family and friends who support me always and have my back!

To Angela, Rachel, Tania, Meghan and Jen who over the years have helped me to piece everything together and connect the dots ....

To Shelley, Paulina, Renee, Rachel and Jo, who inspire me to move every single day.

To the amazing people I work with. Thank you for trusting me. It means so much!

To the beautiful talented artists Rachael Sullivan and Sania Butt, who helped me to bring my words to life. To Jennifer Doohan who managed to capture a perfect photograph and to Lucie, Liv and Joanne for being my other eyes.

Dedicated to the memory of my late father in law Ben, who loved words and books and always expressed how each and everyone has a book within them. Their very own life story. I never believed him until now.

Printed in Poland
by Amazon Fulfillment
Poland Sp. z o.o., Wrocław

24734992R00065